UNDERSTANDING COMPUTER SYSTEMS

OTHER BOOKS OF INTEREST

Wayne Amsbury
Structured Basic and Beyond

M. Carberry, H. Khalil, J. Leathrum, and L. Levy
Foundations of Computer Science

William Findlay and David Watt
Pascal: An Introduction to Methodical Programming

David Levy
Chess and Computers

David Levy and Monroe Newborn
More Chess and Computers: The Microcomputer Revolution
The Challenge Match

Tom Logsdon
Computers and Social Controversy
Computers and Social Controversy Workbook

Ira Pohl and Alan Shaw
The Nature of Computation: An Introduction to Computer Science

UNDERSTANDING COMPUTER SYSTEMS

HAROLD W. LAWSON, JR.
Linköping University, Sweden

COMPUTER SCIENCE PRESS

Printed in the United States of America.

Computer Science Press, Inc.
11 Taft Court.
Rockville, Maryland 20850

2 3 4 5 6 Printing   Year 86 85 84 83

Library of Congress Cataloging in Publication Data

Lawson, Harold W.
Understanding computer systems.

1. Electronic digital computers. I. Title.
QA76.5.L373 1982 001.64'2 81-17295
ISBN 0-914894-31-5 AACR2

Cover design by Ruth Ramminger

PREFACE

The impact of computer systems technology upon the individual and society has steadily increased since the introduction of modern digital computers after World War II. Computers have become more powerful and less expensive and this has led to a widespread governmental, institutional, industrial and business utilization of the technology. In particular, the development of "microcomputers" in the 1970's has resulted in the possibility for small organizations and, in fact, most individuals to own and operate their own computer.

This growing impact most certainly is resulting in a "need to know" more about the technology as well as its impacts upon the citizenry of the world. In Norway, the labor unions have obtained agreements with employer organizations concerning computer based systems. The agreements contain paragraphs that express the **right** of employees to "gain insight into and understand fundamental features of the systems **they themselves use or are affected by** and to understand the importance of the use of such systems both to the company and the employees in their work situation". Further, the agreement states that systems must be explained in a "language easily understood by persons lacking special knowledge of the area concerned". A growing awareness and, in fact, revolutionary attitudes similar to those related to atomic energy can occur in relationship to the widespread utilization of computer based systems, particularly when job replacement by automation occurs. Education based upon an easy to understand approach to computer systems as well as timely, responsible political and socio-economic decisions are essential to achieving a peaceful transition to the automation of organizational activities.

Unfortunately, while major advances in computer systems have been accomplished, corresponding advances in providing for an easy understanding of the technological aspects of computer systems have not been made. Today's systems are, to a large extent, as difficult to understand and utilize as the earliest computers. Computer manufacturer supplied literature, in the form of manuals, are often difficult to understand, particularly for the beginner, and an overview of the computer system as a whole is quite difficult to ascertain. Most textbooks on the subject begin by introducing the details of how the central parts of a computer system work and the reader "student" studies the trees and their leaves instead of first obtaining an overview of the forest.

This book is directed, firstly, to beginners who know nothing or very little about computer systems. The novel approach used here will give the reader "student" an overview of computer based systems including important concepts and terminology. This overview provides a solid platform upon which to study the details of computer technology for those who plan to go further and specialize in the field as well as providing the layman with a well rounded view of the computer technology milieu. Further, the book is directed to those who already have computer technology knowledge as a guide to solidifying the many aspects of the technology as well as providing assistance in educating others.

The book may, for example, be utilized in an introductory course in computer science or computer technology to give a brief but comprehensive overview of what is to come. The book may also be effectively utilized in a computer appreciation course or study-circle since all participants can participate in discussing the subject material directly from the beginning. Teaching assistance materials for utilizing this book in the classroom or in study-circles are available.

I have wanted to write this book for many years and finally, I have found time to collect my thoughts and present them. Any effort of this type is not the work of one individual and I wish to express my thanks to several "interested parties." First, to my many colleagues in many corners of the world from whom I have learned and with whom I have had the opportunity to discuss the novel approach followed in this book. A special thanks to Captain Dr. Grace M. Hopper for providing the starting point for my own base of knowledge in the field of computing. Secondly, to the students and staff at Linkopings University who have read, commented and corrected. Particularly, I would like to thank Rolf Flisberg, Bjorn Gudmundsson, Bengt Johnsson and Erik Tengvald for their very useful comments. Thirdly, to Marianne Anse-Lundberg, Tomas Hedblom, Eleanor Johansson and Lena Hjaellsten who helped with drawing and typing. Fourthly, to Peter Jensen and Richard Eckhouse for providing valuable comments on the first edition of the book. Finally, to Ann and Nadia who provide my inspiration and to whom I dedicate this work.

Happy reading,

Harold W. Lawson, Jr.

TABLE OF CONTENTS

Chapter 1
INTRODUCTION

In attempting to understand the function of computer systems and their utilization, one is faced with many learning difficulties due to the seemingly complicated structure and many intricately interrelated aspects of computer systems. However, in this book we introduce a means of describing computer systems that relates to well-known "real life analogies." By utilizing this associative approach, readers will be able to extend their knowledge of what they already know to include many important computer system concepts and terminology.

In the brief history of digital computer systems (*) there has arisen a need for many types of specialists in the computer field. Unfortunately, as the technology developed, the specialists worked, far too often, in isolation from each other and thus many specialized forms of computer technology related skills developed. This is vividly reflected in the special types of technical "languages" utilized by these specialists in carrying out their work. The interaction of the many technical disciplines required in designing, constructing and utilizing computer systems has led to many complexities. The complexities in computer system structures, the language aspect and the problem of understanding are quite nicely summarized in the following quotation:

> "THE UNIVERSE AND ITS REFLECTION IN THE IDEAS OF MAN HAVE WONDERFULLY COMPLEX STRUCTURES. OUR ABILITY TO COMPREHEND THIS COMPLEXITY AND PERCEIVE AN UNDERLYING SIMPLICITY IS INTIMATELY BOUND WITH OUR ABILITY TO SYMBOLIZE AND COMMUNICATE OUR EXPERIENCE. THE SCIENTIST HAS BEEN FREE TO EXTEND AND INVENT NEW LANGUAGES WHENEVER OLD FORMS BECAME UNWIELDY OR INADEQUATE TO EXPRESS HIS IDEAS. HIS READERS, HOWEVER, HAVE FACED THE DOUBLE TASK OF LEARNING HIS NEW LANGUAGE AND THE STRUCTURES HE DESCRIBED. THERE HAS, THEREFORE, ARISEN A NATURAL CONTROL: **A WORK OF ELABORATE LINGUISTIC INVENTIVENESS AND MEAGER RESULTS WILL NOT BE WIDELY READ.**"
>
> WILLIAM M. McKEEMAN

(*) Note that the first fully electronic digital computer system called ENIAC was designed by J. Presper Eckert and John Mauchly and constructed at the Moore School of Electrical Engineering of the University of Pennsylvania in 1945.

Let us complement this single process by introducing a second process, thus creating a **system** of **cooperating processes.**

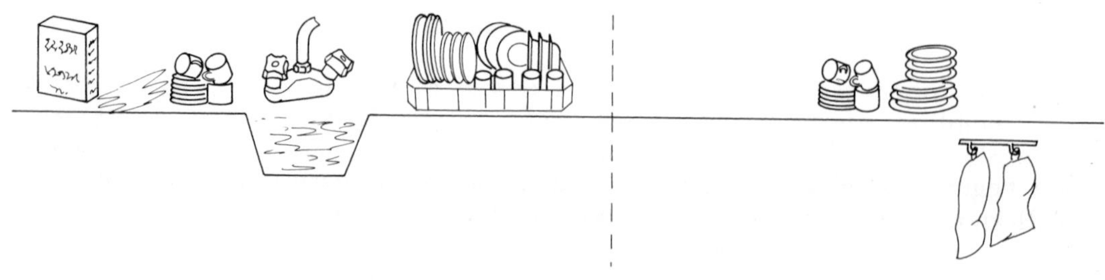

A SECOND PROCESS

Note: Implicit in this description is the definition of a **system** as a collection of interrelated processes.

We can continue the general abstraction of this system of cooperating processes by introducing an abstraction for the second process, namely the drying process, in the following manner:

AN ABSTRACTION OF A SYSTEM OF COOPERATING PROCESSES

If the processes are to be carried out by a single processor, **uni-processor,** then this single processor must be assigned to both the WASH and the DRY process as indicated in the following picture.

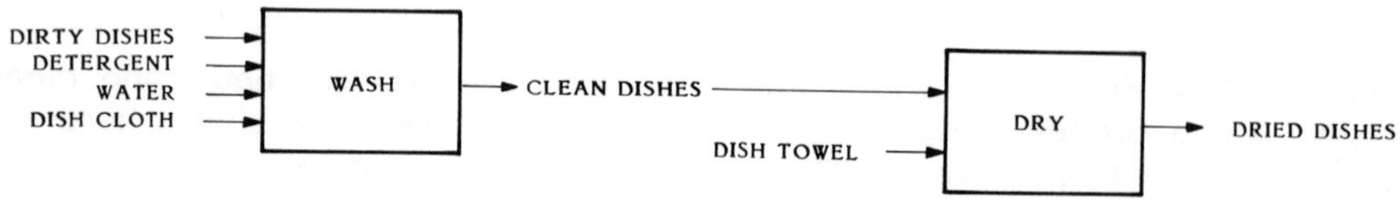

A UNI-PROCESSOR

Note that if the dishrack becomes **full** during WASH execution then the single uni-processor must be alternated between the execution of the processes WASH and DRY. Alternatively, we could assign a processor to each process, that is, the processes are executed **concurrently** (at the same time) by **multi-processors.**

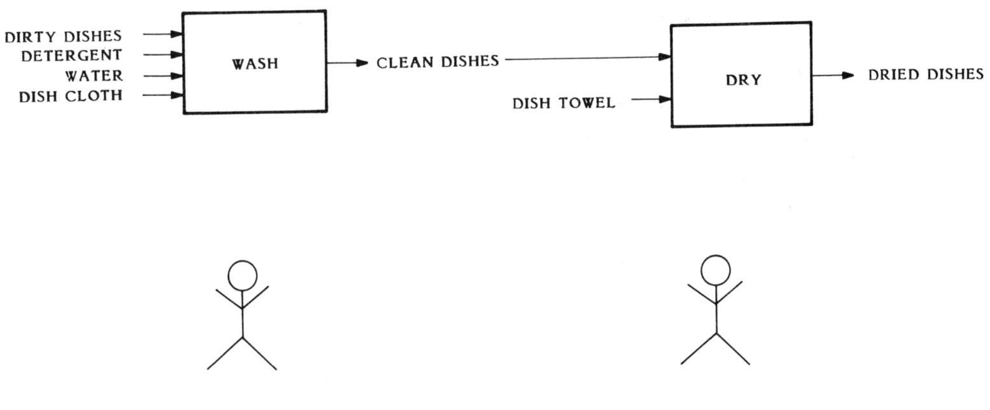

MULTI-PROCESSORS

During execution of a process by a processor, let us say the WASH process, the processor could be **interrupted** by a **higher priority process** such as the following:

A HIGH PRIORITY PROCESS

Consequently, a new process is **"created"** which we can represent abstractly as follows:

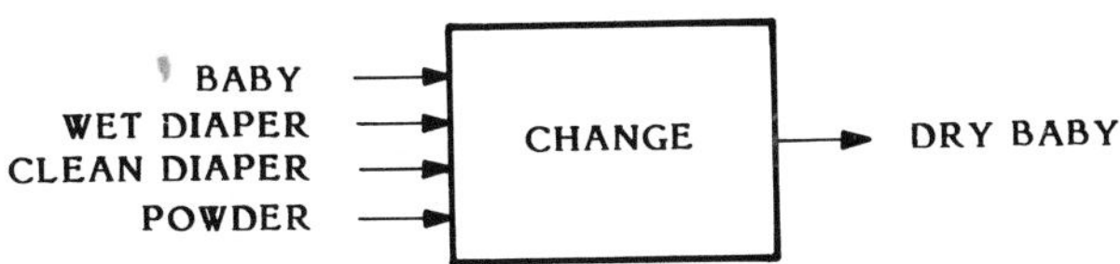

AN ABSTRACTION OF THE NEW PROCESS

In the case of a single uni-processor, the processor temporarily **"suspends"** the process it is currently executing and **"initiates"** execution of the CHANGE process. After **"termination"** of the CHANGE process, the processor returns to **"resumes"** execution of the process that was suspended.

Alternatively, in the case of multi-processors, the processor that acknowledges the interrupt (let us say the processor serving the WASH process) could **"assign"** another processor (the processor assigned to DRY or another available processor) to execute the CHANGE process in **"parallel"** with the ongoing WASH and/or DRY processes as follows:

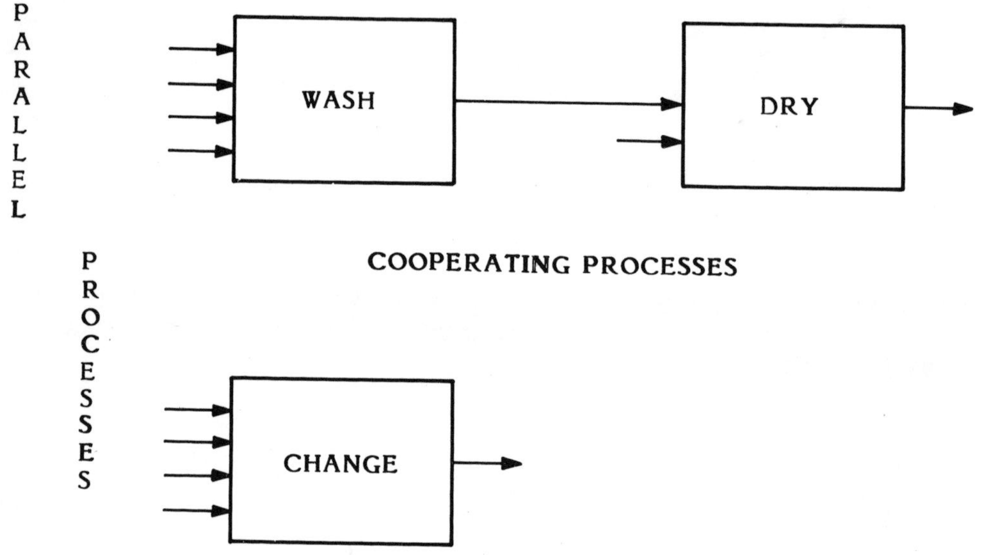

Summary

In summary, thus far, if we have a single processor **uni-processor,** the processor can only be assigned to a single process execution at any given moment. The processor can service one of the **cooperating processes** WASH or DRY or if a higher priority process **interrupt** appears (baby cries due to wet diapers), the processor's attention can be turned to executing a **parallel process,** namely the CHANGE process and when that process is completed, it can resume with the WASH or DRY process execution that was temporarily suspended.

If **multi-processors** (let us say two processors) are available, they could, for example, be assigned to the WASH and DRY **cooperating processes** and one of them could be assigned at the time of **interrupt** to the **parallel process** CHANGE while the other processor can continue serving the WASH and/or DRY process.

Word List

We have now considered some rather non-trivial concepts of well-known processes and systems which have their correlaries in computer systems. Readers should verify their understanding of these concepts by once more relating the following terminology to the examples given and to the problems listed below. Please note once again that process and task, which is indicated in parenthesis (), are synonymous terms.

process (task)	process inputs
process outputs	process execution
processor	system
cooperating processes	uni-processor
concurrent processes	multi-processors
interrupt	process priority
process creation	process suspension
process initiation	process termination
process resumption	processor assignment
parallel processes	

Problems

1. Building upon the previous example:

   a). Extend the picture of the WASH and DRY processes to include a process for TABLE CLEARING and a DISH STORING process.

   b). Extend the abstract description of this system of processes.

   c). Explain how the dishes will be processed through these four processes if only a uni-processor is available to execute processes.

   d). Explain how the dishes can be processed if we have multi-processors, namely, 2, 3 or 4 processors available to assign to execution of the processes.

   e). What happens if the telephone rings while the dishes are being processed, in the case of a uni-processor and in the case of multi-processors?

2. You have been fortunate to receive, as a present, an automatic dishwashing machine.

   a). Create a new picture of the system of processes by replacing the WASH and DRY processes by a new single process WASH/DRY.

   b). Create a new abstract description reflecting this substitution.

   c). Which processor will be applied in executing the WASH/DRY process?

   d). How will the processor initiate the execution of the WASH/DRY process?

WARNING

TO THOSE WHO ONLY HAVE A HAMMER, THE WHOLE WORLD LOOKS LIKE A NAIL.

TO THOSE WHO ONLY KNOW COMPUTERS, THE WHOLE WORLD LOOKS LIKE AN INFORMATION PROCESSING MACHINE.

JOSEPH WEIZENBAUM

We have utilized well known real life processes to illustrate some important computer related concepts. It would be a disastrous mistake to assume that all real life processes and systems can be computerized. Our real life natural processes and many processes developed by people and related to individuals and their environment are far too sophisticated and complex to be accurately computerized in every real detail.

Unfortunately, as Weizenbaum suggests, many computing professionals, due to their perspective, narrow their view of the world and try to view everything in terms of equivalents of "computerized" processes and systems. This viewpoint is **not** to be taken by the readers of this book.

With these warnings in mind, let us proceed with obtaining an understanding of computer systems via pictures and real life analogies.

Chapter 3

PROCESS AND SYSTEM "DATA" FLOW

A primary goal of **information** processing systems is to process **data.** But what is **information** and what is **data**? For a definition of data, let us consider the following quotation:

> "DATA: A REPRESENTATION OF FACTS OR IDEAS IN A FORMALIZED MANNER CAPABLE OF BEING COMMUNICATED OR MANIPULATED BY SOME PROCESS."
>
> PETER NAUR

Data as alluded to by Naur is simply a representation of something; whereas, **information** is an interpretation given to data in some well defined context. The numbers (6, 3, 1, 12, 9) are data representations but they only become information when we know what they represent; for example, apples, age, meters, etc.. This point is often confusing and we see references to both **information processing systems** and **data processing systems.** It is a matter of taste as to which term best describes the use of computer systems in processing data/information. We shall utilize the term **information processing system** in this book.

Our real life analogy of the previous chapter is a **dish processing system** in which we deal with real objects instead of representations. However, in continuing our analogy, we shall treat these objects as being counterparts to data in an information processing system.

In formalizing the notion of objects (data) for our dish processing system, let us concentrate only upon the dishes (ignoring detergent, water, etc.) to be processed through the entire system. In order to describe and enumerate all of the possible "types" of dishes that can be processed, we build an **alphabet** of dishes. This alphabet along with an illustrative picture of the objects (data) entering and leaving the WASH process is as follows:

ALPHABET OF DISHES {CUP, SAUCER, SALAD DISH, MEAT DISH}

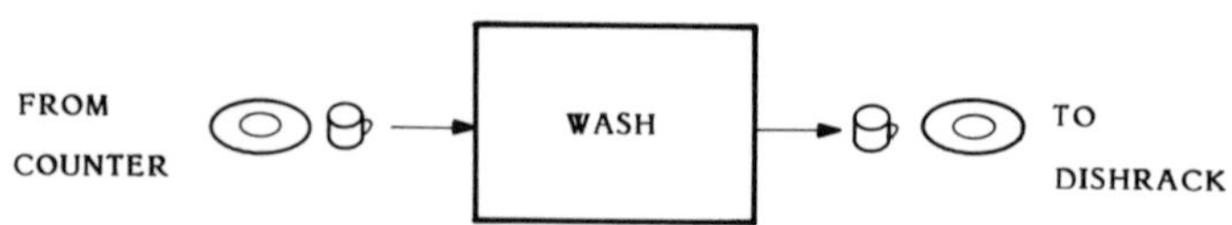

ENUMERATION OF PROCESS RELATED OBJECTS (DATA)

Alphabets in the case of this formalism restrict the type of objects (data) that can be processed by a process. This is completely analogous to the notion of an alphabet in a natural language, let us say English with its 26 letters (A to Z) which then restricts our "word construction process" to using only these 26 alphabet members.

When the objects (data) are processed by a process, they frequently go through a rather standard 3 step cycle which we illustrate in general terms and concretely in terms of the WASH process.

PROCESS STEPS	WASH PROCESS STEPS
input object (data)	take object from counter
processing of object (data)	wash object
output object (data)	place object in dishrack

Now that we have considered the basic concepts of the alphabet of process objects (data) and their flow through a process, let us ask the question: where are the process objects (data) taken from (input) and where are they placed (output)? In the previous picture and process step description, we note that they are taken from a counter and they are placed in the dishrack. Thus the counter and the dishrack are **storages** which hold objects (data) to be processed and during process execution, objects (data) are taken from a storage for processing and placed in a storage after processing. In the following picture, we show an abstraction of the storages, processes and object (data) flow in our system for dish processing.

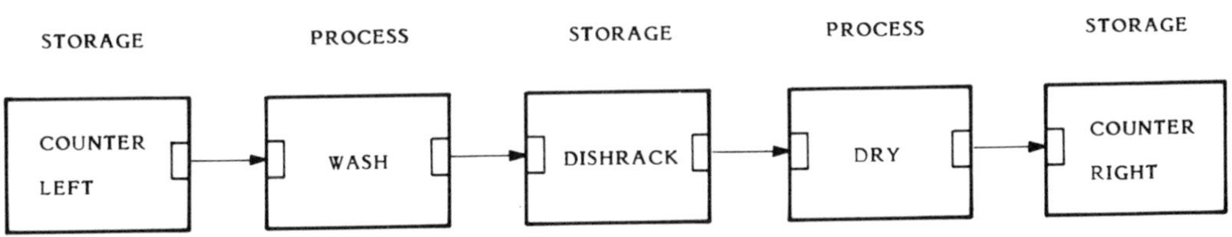

STORAGES, PROCESSES AND OBJECT (DATA) FLOW

In this new version of our model of the dish processing system where only the flow of objects (data) of the type dishes is illustrated, we assume that the same alphabet of dishes is "known" to and used by all storages and processes in the system. That is, the processes are restricted to processing the same type of dishes.

The small boxes at the entry and exit points of the processes and storages are used to represent **ports** where objects (data) are received at and sent from the processes or storage. The terms **input port** and **output port** are naturally derived from the function of the port within the process or storage. The reader may make an anology to airports or harbor ports. Namely, they are places at which objects may enter and/or leave a process, in these two cases, transportation processes. A loading platform is yet another good example of a port.

From the dish processing example, we can observe that **storage is a process** that has a special function of being a temporary holding place for objects (data) to be processed. We may therefore utilize the term **storage process** which includes the physical storage as a component. The reader, in this case, may make the analogy to a waiting room in an airport or to a warehouse at the harbor.

We may ask the further question: how are objects (data) transmitted between storages and processes and vice versa? When we wash or dry dishes, we take the objects from a storage port with our arms and hands under control, of course, of our eyes, brain and nervous system. However, to make our real life model appear more like a computer related system, we should think that the actual **transmission** of objects (data) between the ports of storages and processes takes place over a **channel** which is analogous to a moving sidewalk in an airport or a conveyor belt used to transport to and from a warehouse. A partial picture of our dish processing system with transmission channels is shown in the following picture:

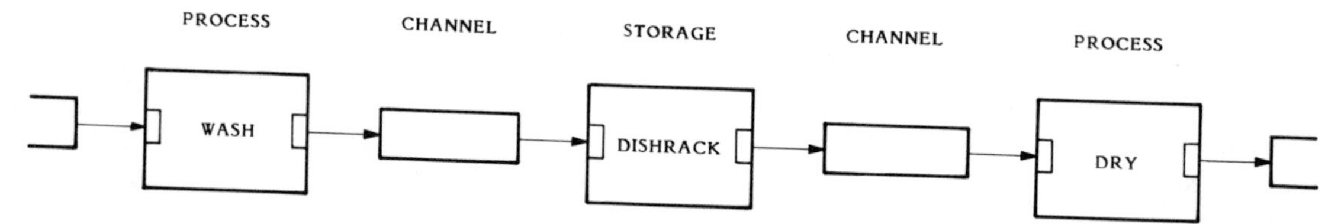

TRANSMISSION OF OBJECTS (DATA) OVER CHANNELS

In the example we have considered, the path of dish processing is only in one direction through the various processes of the system. When a channel only permits transmission in a single direction, the transmission mode is called **simplex.** However, it is possible, and often required, to have channels which permit transmission in both directions. In this case the transmission mode is called **duplex** or **half-duplex.** These three transmission possibilities are illustrated as follows:

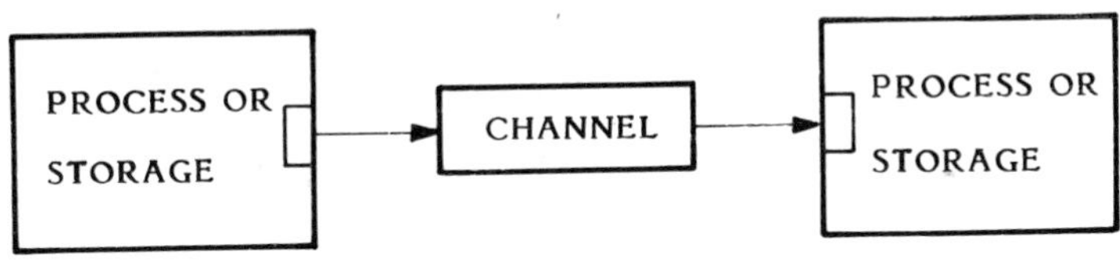

SIMPLEX TRANSMISSION

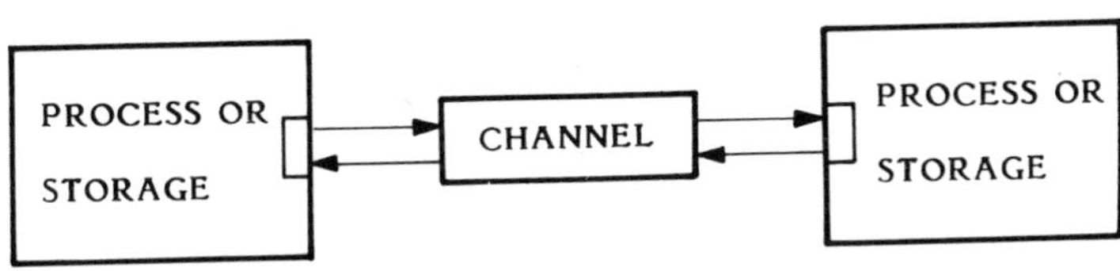

DUPLEX TRANSMISSION

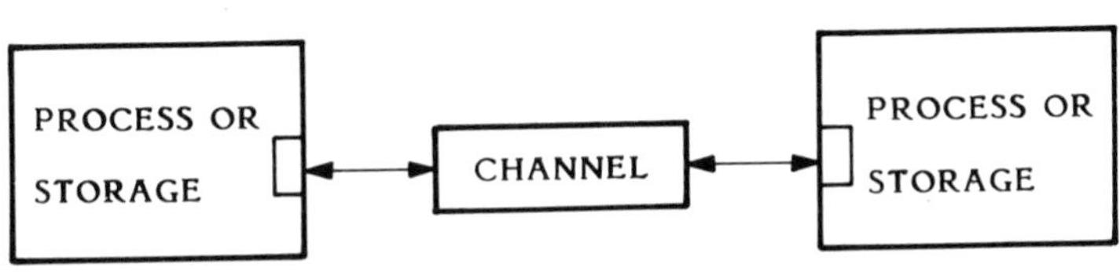

HALF-DUPLEX TRANSMISSION

Notice that in the case of a duplex transmission, the process or storage has both input ports and output ports which are connected to the channel. Again, the reader can make the analogy to a conveyor belt designed to transport in only one direction (simplex) and the use of two conveyor belts side-by-side for transporting in opposite directions simultaneously (duplex). A conveyor belt whose direction can be reversed, thus permitting transport in two directions but **not** simultaneously exemplifies half-duplex transmission.

In our dish processing example, we have assumed only simplex transmission. We could, however, quickly realize the need for duplex or half-duplex transmission. Consider a case where it is determined that a previously washed dish is to be returned to the WASH process to be rewashed.

Summary

In summary, **data** is a formalized representation of facts or ideas; whereas, **information** is an interpretation given to data in a well defined context. Both terms **information processing system** and **data processing system** are derived from this definition. In formalizing a data representation, we enumerate the "types" of objects (data) in the form of an **alphabet.** Objects (data) are normally cycled through a process in 3 distinct steps (input, processing, output). When objects (data) are not currently under processing by a process, they can be contained in **storages.** Objects (data) are received at and sent from **ports** of processes or storages. Storages are contained in a special type of process which we have named **storages processes.** The movement of objects (data) in the system between processes and storages and vice versa is termed **transmission** and transmission occurs over **channels.** The channel can be constructed to permit **simplex** (single direction), **duplex** or **half-duplex** transmission, the latter two being bi-directional.

Word List

Our knowledge of computer concepts and terminology has now been further extended and the readers should verify their knowledge of these new concepts and terms by reviewing the examples given and applying this knowledge to the problems listed below.

data	information
information processing system	data processing system
alphabet	storage
port	input port
output port	storage process
transmission	channels
simplex	duplex
half-duplex	

Problems

1. Extend the alphabet of dishes given in this chapter to include a KNIFE, a FORK and a SPOON.

2. Build upon the extended dish processing system example from the previous chapter including the TABLE CLEARING and DISH STORING processes.

   a). Using an adequately large piece of paper, introduce the storage processes where objects are taken from and placed.

   b). Describe the steps of input, processing and output for each of the processes in processing dishes through the system.

   c). Extend the model to include process and storage input and output ports and transmission channels with simplex transmission between the storages and processes.

   d). A dish is determined to be not adequately clean during the DISH STORING process. How can the dish be returned to the WASH process?

3. Using your imagination, draw a simplified picture and an abstract model of the check-in hall, check-in counter, a boarding area and a plane at an airport. Illustrate the ports and transmission channels where the objects (people) enter and leave the various processes and are transmitted between processes.

4. Again using your imagination, draw a simplified picture and an abstract model of a ship, dock and warehouse at a harbor. Illustrate the ports and transmission channels where the objects (goods) enter and leave ports and are transmitted between processes.

Chapter 4
CONTROL OF PROCESSING IN A SYSTEM OF PROCESSES

Let us begin by defining what is meant by "control" of processing in a system.

> **Control** is that system function which "coordinates" the activities of the processors as they service (execute) the processes of the system. The coordination involves the responsibility for assuring that the process activities are in "synchronization" with respect to **time.**

Control in this definition can easily be compared with the function of a project manager who plans the activities of the various parts (processes) of a project and then provides control (i.e. time synchronization) of project (system) execution by scheduling the use of available personnel (processors). The project manager can utilize a variety of strategies for realizing the control function.

In the environment of computer systems, the control function is analogous to the activities of the project manager. Two main strategies or approaches to control process execution in a system of computer processes are as follows:

> **asynchronous control** which attempts to achieve a degree of **speed (time) independence** of the rate of individual process execution.

and

> **synchronous control** which requires that the rate of individual process execution is completely **speed (time) dependent** in respect to the synchronization of all activities in the system.

An important mechanism in realizing control under the asynchronous or synchronous strategy is the use of **signals.** Basically, the control function utilizes **signals** to indicate "when" something is to happen or "when" something has gone wrong. The signalling of processes is illustrated in the following picture in which the start signals tell the processes when to begin and the reset signals are related to **error conditions** (something has gone wrong).

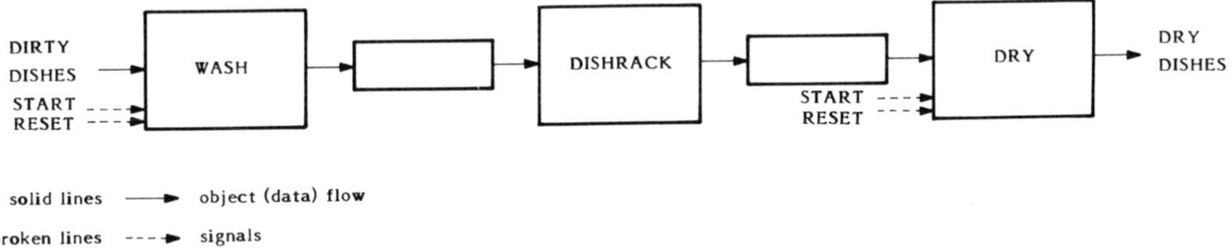

SIGNALS FROM THE CONTROL FUNCTION

Note that solid lines are used to denote data flow; whereas, broken lines are utilized to denote signals. Further, we have dispensed with the explicit denotation of ports in the process boxes. A port's existence is implied by a **data** or **signal** connection to the process.

Signals play an important role in the use of our earlier analogy of the control function and the project manager. The signals used by the project manager can include time schedules, memorandums, reminders, etc. delivered to the subprojects and which are to be acted upon "executed" by the human processors that are executing that subproject. Let us now return to the dish processing system to explain the concepts and terminology related to asynchronous control, synchronous control, signals and other related control functions.

Asynchronous Control

In the previous chapter, we introduced the notion of storage processes into our dish processing system. Storage processes have some important impacts upon the realization of asynchronous control of processes in the system. A storage on the counter or the dishrack provides a **buffer** between processes in the system. For example, after dishes are processed in the WASH process, they are transmitted over a channel to the DISHRACK storage process. They are further transmitted over a channel to the DRY process. The DISHRACK storage process provides the required **buffering** between the WASH and DRY processes.

The use of buffers is extremely important when we consider the introduction of asynchronism (time independence) into our model. The rate of speed of process execution is obviously dependent upon the capabilities of the processor that is supplied to execute the process (various people "human processors" wash and dry dishes at different speeds) and further upon any **"system constraints"** placed upon execution. One such constraint is the size "capacity" of the buffer storage. As was illustrated in a previous chapter, when the DISHRACK buffer becomes full, the WASH process must be delayed "wait" until the DRY process causes the removal of some dishes from the DISHRACK buffer.

If only a uni-processor is available, this means that the control function is quite simple. The processor must be reassigned to the DRY process and some dishes must be processed there (dried), before the processor can continue the WASH process.

When multi-processors are available, the cooperating processes can be executed in parallel. The use of buffers leads to the possibility of having a degree of **speed independence** of process execution. A **producing process,** (serviced "executed" by one processor) WASH in this case, can produce process outputs faster than DRY, a **consuming process** (being serviced by another processor) can **consume** them as process inputs. This situation is illustrated in the following picture.

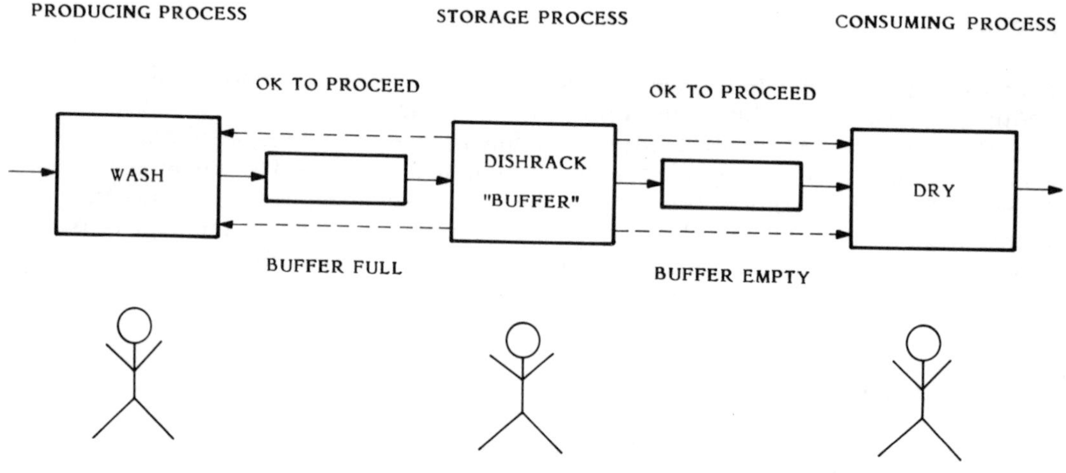

ASYNCHRONOUS CONTROL OF MULTI-PROCESSORS

In this picture, we introduce signals emanating from the storage process DISHRACK acting as a buffer between the WASH and DRY processes. Observe that the storage process DISHRACK has also been assigned a processor since **all** processes need a processor in order to be executed.

We assume that the processes have been started and are in operation. The concept of asynchronism is now best illustrated by the following description of the actions of the DISHRACK process in which the reader should imagine playing the role of the processor serving this storage process.

The DISHRACK process receives requests from the WASH process every time WASH wishes to output (produce) an object (data) into the dishrack. If there is sufficient room in the dishrack, the object is placed there for eventual processing by the DRY process; **otherwise,** the DISHRACK process **signals** the WASH process to **wait** due to a **full** dishrack "buffer". The WASH process must **wait** until the DRY process requests to consume objects (data) of sufficient size so that the newly produced object can be accommodated in the dishrack. At this point, the DISHRACK process **signals** the WASH process that it is **OK to proceed.**

Further, the DISHRACK process receives requests from the DRY process every time it wishes to input (consume) an object (data) from the dishrack. If there are no objects (data) in the dishrack, the DISHRACK process **signals** the DRY process to wait due to an **empty** dishrack "buffer". The DRY process must wait until the WASH process produces objects (data). At this point, the DISHRACK process **signals** the DRY process that it is **OK to proceed.**

The storage process DISHRACK provides an important service for the WASH and DRY processes to utilize. The dishrack that the DISHRACK process **"owns"** and administers is called a **resource.** Further, the administration of this storage resource and subsequent control of WASH and DRY process progress leads us to the notion that the DISHRACK process, in addition to being a **storage process,** is a **monitor process** that "monitors" the use of the dishrack resource. Therefore, the DISHRACK process is in a position to "control" the activities of the WASH and DRY processes by enforcing limitations based upon system constraints (capacity of the dishrack in this case).

The question of **resource ownership** (that is, who owns a resource) in asynchronously controlled systems is extremely important for achieving an "independence" of processes. To illustrate this point, we can consider the partitioning of our dish processing system in such a manner that the dishrack belongs to (is owned by) the WASH process or by the DRY process. That is, the buffer storage is contained within the process instead of being a separate process. The implications of these resource ownerships are illustrated in the following picture.

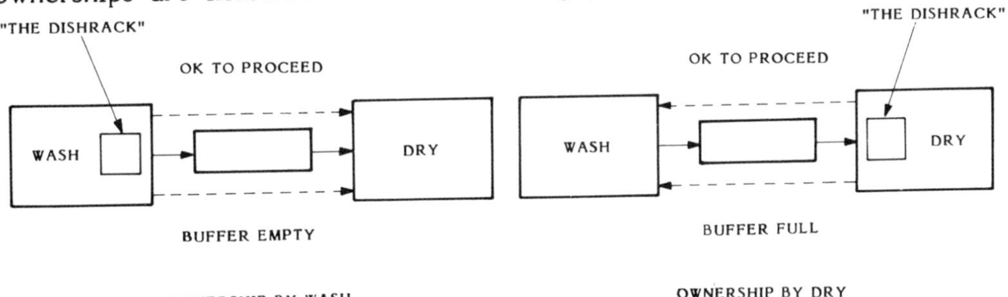

IMPLICATIONS OF RESOURCE OWNERSHIP

One can quickly observe that the process that owns the resource is the process that is in control. It controls the progress of the other process. Notice, in the case of ownership by the producing process WASH that a signal for the buffer empty condition is required. Whereas, when ownership is in the consuming process, a signal for the full buffer condition is required.

This question of ownership may seem arbitrary and unimportant; however, it is a very important issue in the context of computer related systems. When we utilized a separate DISHRACK **monitor process** and gave ownership of the dishrack resource to this process, we took away control from the WASH or DRY process.

Let us say that we decide to install a larger or smaller dishrack then the one currently in use. If the dishrack is owned by WASH or DRY, then we must go in and alter the structure of the owning process so that it "knows" the capacity of the new dishrack. However, if the DISHRACK monitor process owns the resource, we change the knowledge in this process without having to alter the WASH or DRY processes. WASH and DRY operate in this environment "independent" of the size "capacity" of the buffer provided by the DISHRACK process.

In a larger system of processes with several monitor processes, we observe that the question of controlling progress in the system is delegated to the monitors. Individual processors in serving processes can operate at full capacity up to the limits of the **system constraints** imposed by the monitors. Further, we observe that under asynchronous control, signals are utilized to control process progression.

Synchronous Control

To illustrate the concept of synchronous control, let us assume that a dishrack is not available as an intermediary "buffer" between the WASH and DRY processes. That is, there is no storage in which dishes under processing can be held temporarily. The WASH process, after washing a dish, outputs the dish onto the channel, where the DRY process can input the dish, dry the dish and output the dried dish to the counter. At the exact same time that the dish is being dried by the DRY process, the WASH process can input a new dish and wash the dish. At most one object (data) can be processed by each process simultaneously. Further, the progress of the processes is strictly controlled by a common timing mechanism which tells the processes exactly when they are to start their input, processing, output cycles for each object (data) to be processed as illustrated in the following picture.

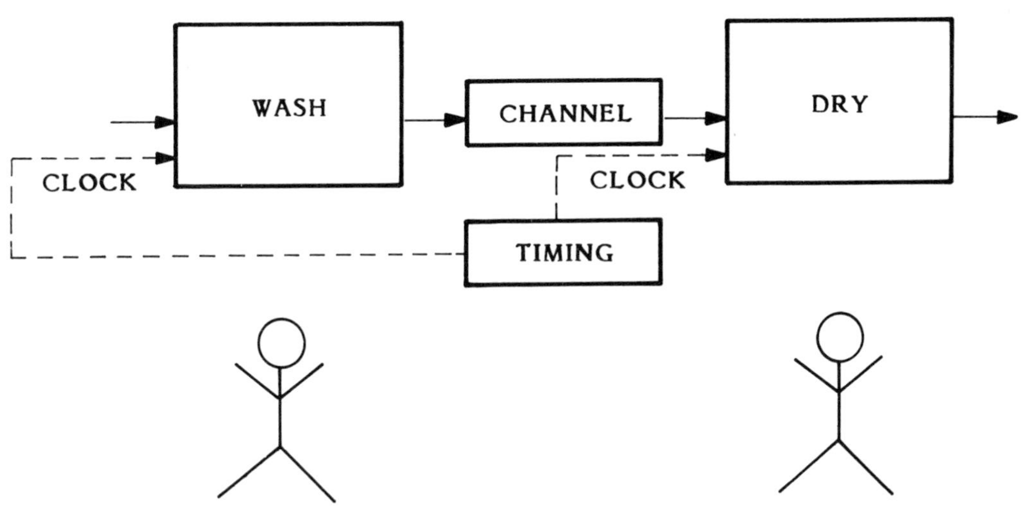

SYNCHRONOUS CONTROL OF MULTI-PROCESSORS

The timing is provided in the form of a **clock signal** given simultaneously to both processes. Each process **must** wash or dry one dish before the clock signal is given again. For example, the clock signal could be given every 10 seconds. This 10 second limit is then to be obeyed by each process. Let us say that the WASH process normally takes between 6 and 8 seconds with 10 seconds as a "worst case". Further, the DRY process usually takes between 3 and 5 seconds with a worst case of 7 seconds. With these conditions, the clock signal rate must be set to 10 seconds while reserve capacity in the DRY process is not utilized.

We now see the reason for our earlier classification of synchronous control as being **speed (time) dependent.** From this description of synchronous control, we can observe the following additional characteristics.

Synchronous control implies that multi-processors are utilized.

Synchronous control implies that the rate of speed of processing in the system is determined by the speed of the slowest process execution (that is, the worst case).

Synchronous control implies a strict centralization of the control function based upon providing exact timing via a clock signal.

Additional Control Functions

While the use of asynchronous or synchronous techniques represents an important strategical decision for the control function, there are other control activities which must be taken into account when planning the control function. For example, consider the following questions.

> How are processes to be **initialized** (prepared for execution)?
>
> How are processes to be started?
>
> How will processes indicate that something has gone wrong and how will the control function react when something has gone wrong?

These are important issues which must be solved independently of whether the asynchronous or synchronous strategy is utilized. The methods of realizing these control functions will, of course, differ based upon this selection of timing strategy. The details of realizing these control functions under the two strategies is outside of the scope of this book; however, let us consider the following analogy in order to gain an understanding of the nature of these control functions.

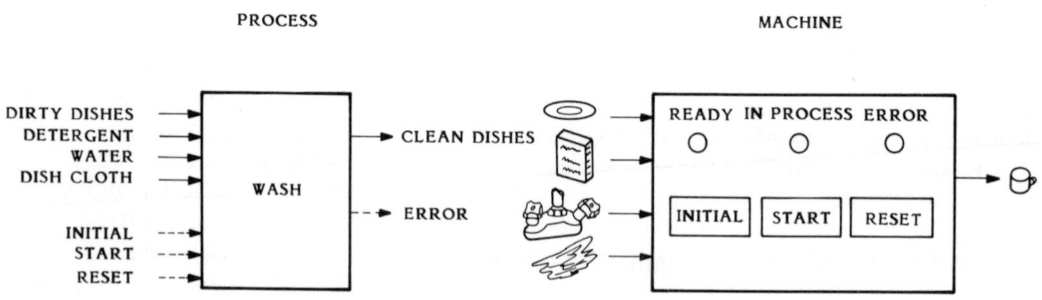

A PROCESS AS A MACHINE CONTROLLED BY PUSH-BUTTONS

We can think of a process, the WASH process in this case, as being a "machine". The signals used to control the process can be thought of as push-buttons on the machine. The machine has three lights which are utilized to show the **"state"** of the machine (process). The machine (process) can go through several states depending upon the control functions exercised (buttons pushed), the resulting actions taken and special conditions that may arise during processing. For the current machine (process), the following states can be observed.

FUNCTION or CONDITION	ACTIONS TAKEN	RESULTING STATE
Initial	Fill basin with water Add detergent Place dish cloth in basin	Ready light lit
Start	Repeat the sequence take dish wash dish place dish	In process light lit
"error"	Depends on error type	Error light lit

The reader undoubtedly has a feeling for what these types of control functions mean in the context of utilizing the many machines that we have in the home, at work and in our recreation.

Summary

In summary, **control** is the system function that coordinates the activities of the processes of a system as they are executed by the available processors. The coordination must be made in respect to time. **Asynchronous control** in which a degree of **speed (time) independence** is achieved for process execution and **synchronous control** in which process execution is entirely **speed (time) dependent** are the two basic control strategies. **Signals** sent to processes are utilized in both of these strategies to realize control over the processes. Further, signals may be given from the processes when they detect an **error conditon** during processing.

In realizing asynchronous control, the use of a **buffer** storage between processes is an important characteristic. The size of the buffer is a good example of a so-called **system constraint** that limits the freedom of process execution under asynchronous control. The two processes that are cooperating in the sending and receiving of objects (data) are called the **producing process** and the **consuming process.** A buffer as well as being a storage, as mentioned in the previous chapter, is a valuable **resource** that is owned and administered by a **monitor process.** The question of **resource ownership** is an important issue since it determines who (what process) is the controlling process.

Under synchronous control, the execution pace is tightly controlled by a central timing mechanism which delivers **clock signals** to the processes. The frequency of the clock signal must be determined based upon the slowest executing process in the system (worst case) and processes that are executed faster must simply wait for clock signals.

In addition to the two major strategies of asynchronous and synchronous control, there are further control functions that must be realized. The control delivers signals to processes and receives signals from processes for these purposes. **Process initialization** is an example of a control function as well as the earlier mentioned **error condition.** A process with its data flow and control flow signals may be likened to a "machine" where the control activities are executed by "push-button" control. Further, the **process (machine) state** is an indication of the current activities of the machine (process).

Word List

Once again, readers should verify their knowledge of the concepts and terms introduced in this chapter by reviewing the examples given and applying this knowledge to the problems listed below.

control
speed (time) independent
speed (time) dependent
error conditions
system constraints
consuming process
monitor process
clock signal
process (machine) state
asynchronous control
synchronous control
signals
buffer
producing process
resource
resource ownership
process initialization

Problems

1. Build upon the extended dish processing example of the previous two chapters which includes the TABLE CLEARING and DISH STORING processes.

    a). Show how asynchronous control with appropriate signals for the **empty** and **full** conditions can be introduced into all intermediate storage processes, thus making them monitor processes that own a resource (i.e. counter space and dishrack).

    b). Describe the effect of having a single uni-processor to assign to the execution of processes in this asynchronous system.

    c). Describe the effect of having two processors for the asynchronous execution.

    d). Describe the effect of utilizing a processor for each process, including the monitor processes.

    e). What system constraints result from having different capacities for the storages?

    f). What is the effect of limiting each storage (counter space and dishrack) to a capacity of one dish at a time?

    g). Make a new version of the dish processing system that only contains channels (no storages) which have capacities of one dish each and a central timing mechanism that delivers synchronous clock signals to each process.

    h). Compare the effect of execution using (g) with the effect resulting from (f).

2. Construct a picture of the DRY process in the form of a "machine" with push buttons for initial, start and reset and lights for ready, in process and error. List the control functions or conditions, actions taken and resulting states for this machine (process).

3. Use your imagination and draw a picture of a coffee dispensing automat in the form of a machine with push buttons and lights. Describe the control functions or conditions, actions taken and resulting states associated with this machine. Note: leave out sugar and cream options in order to simplify the automat. To further simplify the automat, assume that a single coin is required.

Chapter 5
PROCESS LOGIC AND PROGRAMS

The notion of a process as a "machine" that was introduced in the previous chapter has important implications for how we view the internal structure of a process. In particular, the **process (machine) state** is an up-to-date reflection of the progress of the process. The state changes based upon the execution of control functions and the processing of objects (data). These changes of state are called **state transitions.** The possible state transitions for a process can be conveniently represented in a so-called **state transition diagram** which clearly shows the possible states and the reasons for moving from one state to another as follows:

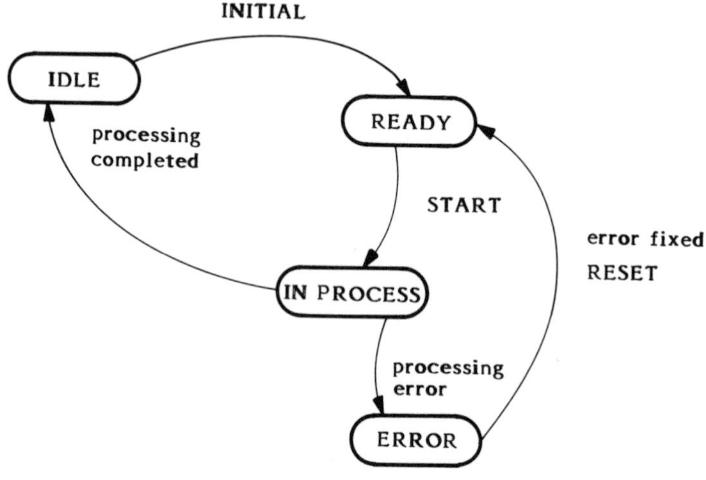

STATE TRANSITION DIAGRAM

Here we see that prior to the initial button (signal) being depressed, the machine (process) is in an IDLE state. After initialization, the machine is placed in READY state. When the start button (signal) is depressed, the machine (process) is placed in the IN PROCESS state and processing begins. From the IN PROCESS state, we can again enter the IDLE state when all processing is completed or the ERROR state if an error is encountered in processing. After the error is fixed, the machine (process) can return to the READY state as a result of the reset button (signal) being depressed. Processing can then be started again by depression of the start button (signal). The number of states in a process (machine) is always limited "finite". Consequently, such processes (machines) are called **finite state machines.**

The state of the process (machine) must be indicated (noted) in some manner inside the process (machine). In order to maintain this record of the state, we can utilize some **local storage** inside of the process in which the state is marked. In our machine like picture from the previous chapter, we can think of the lights for READY, IN PROCESS and ERROR being lit or not lit based upon this status information. The state objects (data) of the WASH process are indicated in the following picture.

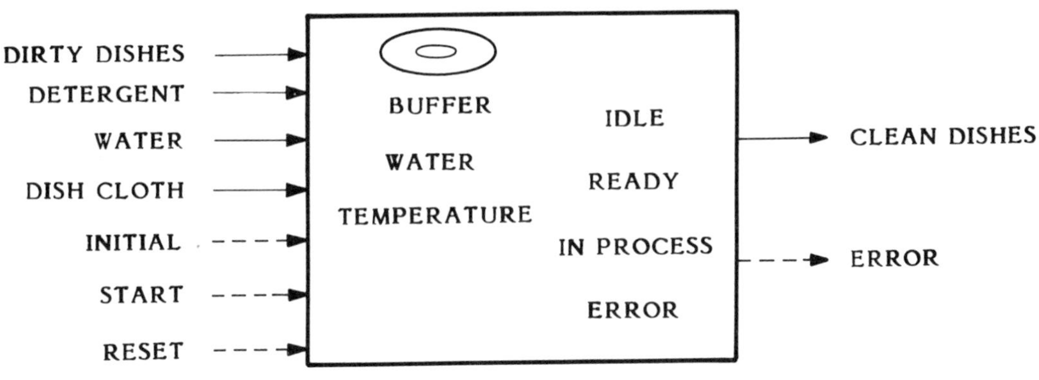

THE STATE OBJECTS (DATA) OF A PROCESS

The **local storage** of the process here which reflects the state of the process consists of the **state indicators** IDLE, READY, IN PROCESS and ERROR, the state of a **local buffer** (BUFFER) which holds objects (data) which have been accessed (input) into the process and are currently being processed and, finally, a measurement of the WATER TEMPERATURE. All of these local objects (data) in computer related terms are called **state variables.** They are variables because at various points in time, they can have different **values.**

From this example, we can observe that all variables local to the process which are utilized in realizing the process belong to the **process state.** Thus, our earlier example of the **monitor process** DISHRACK used in asynchronously controlling the WASH and DRY processes also has a process state which we can represent as follows:

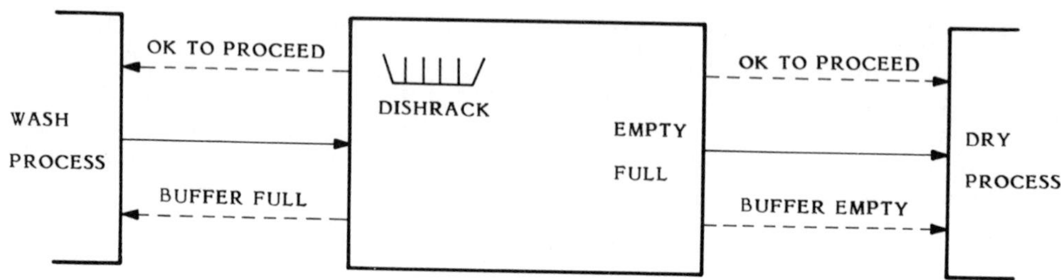

THE STATE OBJECTS (DATA) OF A MONITOR PROCESS

Here we see the state variable indicators EMPTY and FULL as well as the variable dishrack buffer which is "owned" by (i.e. local to) the DISHRACK process.

The logic of a process is the "plan" utilized to specify the execution of the process when a processor is applied. That is, how the process will progress through various states including the details of how processing will occur.

The logic of a process is normally carried out (executed) by we **human processors** according to learned intuition about the order **"sequence"** of actions required to complete the process. We are capable of recognizing normal and abnormal conditions and thus **"selecting"** amongst alternative paths of action. Further, we are capable of taking a complex problem and **"refining"** it into simpler composite paths of action.

The basic aspects of **sequence, selection and refinement** are the backbone of process logic; whether it be the real life process examples that we have considered or processes to be realized in a computer system environment. The planning and realization of process logic, of course, is what we call **"programming"**. When **programs** are planned for a computer system, they must be precise, since the **interpreter** of the program will be a computer system processor that is **not** endowed with human powers of understanding and reasoning. Humans as processors can make less precise **interpretations** of instructions; whereas computer processors stupidly obey only precise instructions.

The nature of a program has been likened to a recipe for cooking or knitting instructions. In fact one of the earliest uses of programming was in the textile industry, namely, the mechanical processor known as the Jacquard loom which needed "instructions" to execute the weaving process.

A further good example of a programmed mechanical device is the player piano which responds to instructions on a song roll with "encoded" music. The **encoding** is represented by holes in well defined positions of the roll that are translated into musical notes by the interpreting processor, namely the player piano. We shall, of course, illustrate process logic for various portions of our dish processing system.

Another common expression for constructing instruction sequences which has historical connection to mathematical procedures in the ancient days of the Arabic Empire is the term **algorithm.** The term algorithm has become almost synonymous with the term program and we shall treat them as being synonymous in this book.

Long before the invention of computers, people developed means of graphically representing the logic of processes. Various forms of **flowdiagrams** or **flowcharts** were introduced as a means of abstractly representing the flow of process logic. Further, many variations of flowcharting techniques and conventions have been presented for the abstract representation of the precise instructions of a computer program. Let us return to the three basic concepts of **sequence, selection and refinement** and their representation in an abstract graphic form which will improve our ability to understand process logic in the form of a program.

The specification of a **sequence** of operations provides us with an ordering, namely, **do this action, then that action, then that action, etc..** We can relate this sequence to the WASH process in the following manner.

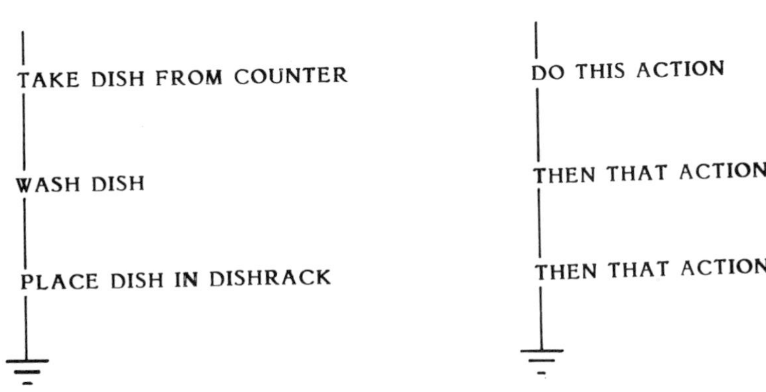
TAKE DISH FROM COUNTER
WASH DISH
PLACE DISH IN DISHRACK
DO THIS ACTION
THEN THAT ACTION
THEN THAT ACTION
NOTE: denotes the termination point for a sequence

A SEQUENCE

Observe the use of a special grounding symbol which indicates the termination point of a sequence of actions.

In order to execute alternative actions, we must be able to make **selections** based upon existing conditions and relationships. Questions called **predicates** can be evaluated and alternative paths specified. We formulate selection by postulating the **existence** of the predicate and the action to be followed; **in case of predicate, do this action.**

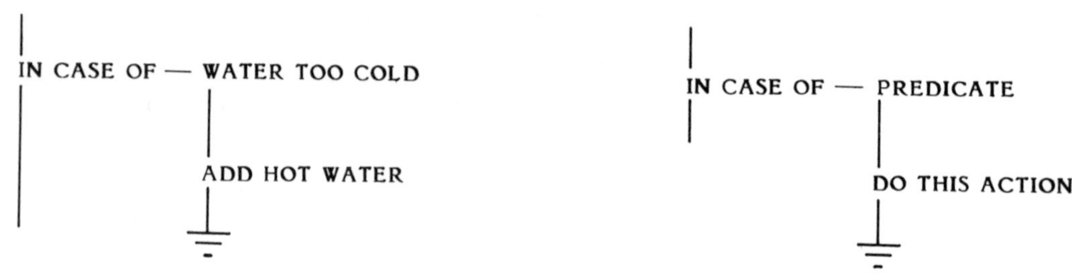
IN CASE OF — WATER TOO COLD
ADD HOT WATER
IN CASE OF — PREDICATE
DO THIS ACTION

A SELECTION

The predicate, in this case, asks if the condition "water too cold" exists by checking the condition of the WATER TEMPERATURE state variable. Of course, the condition "water too cold" is a non-precise condition of which a human processor is capable of making a judgement. However, in the precise environment of computer processors, we would be required to ask the question (predicate) in a more precise manner by stating the predicate, for example, in the form of "water less than a certain temperature".

Perhaps there are several predicates which should be considered and depending upon the existence of a **case,** an action path is selected. That is, **in case of predicate 1, do this sequence; in case of predicate 2, do that sequence; etc..** Thus, we may want to postulate several predicates for our WASH example with the following structure.

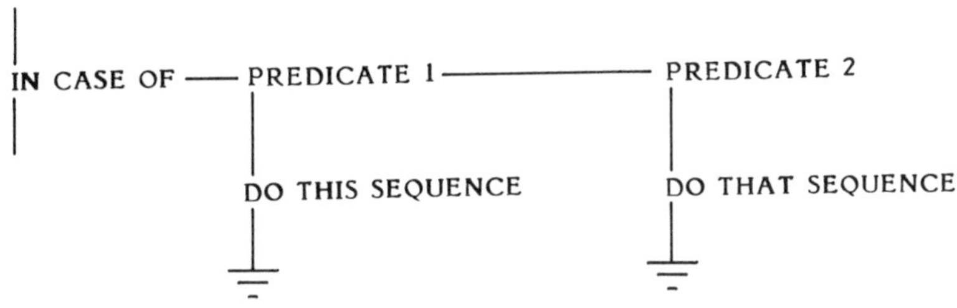

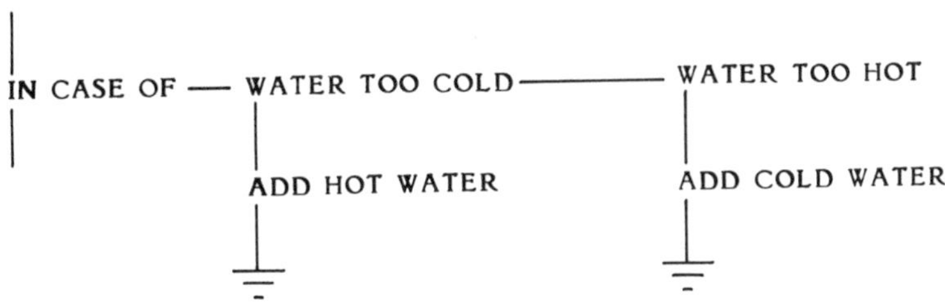

SELECTION BASED UPON MULTIPLE PREDICATES

In addition to sequence and selection, the refinement of program logic from larger composite actions into smaller components is an essential aspect of the programmers job. We can illustrate this need in terms of the types of actions required in initializing the WASH process in response to the initial signal (button pushing) as the following flowchart:

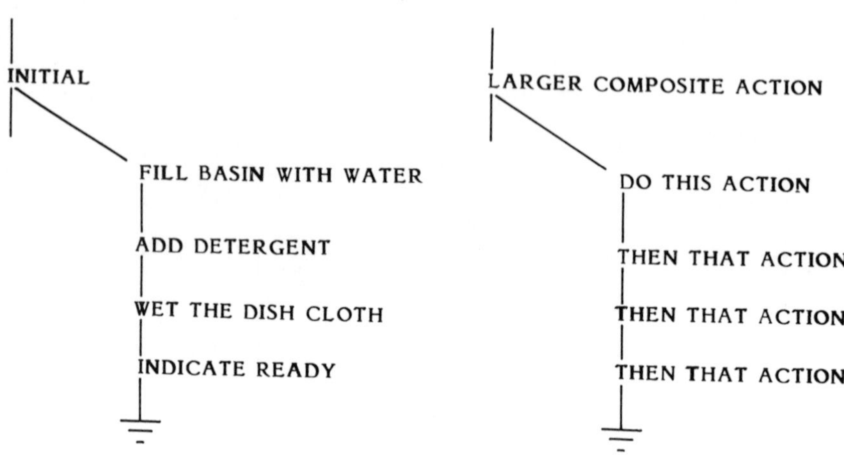
INITIAL
FILL BASIN WITH WATER
ADD DETERGENT
WET THE DISH CLOTH
INDICATE READY
LARGER COMPOSITE ACTION
DO THIS ACTION
THEN THAT ACTION
THEN THAT ACTION
THEN THAT ACTION

A REFINEMENT

We have observed that the three basic components of sequence, selection and refinement are represented in our flowchart form by denoting three directions, vertical (for sequence), horizontal (for selection) and diagonal (for refinement) which we show as flowcharting conventions in summary form as follows:

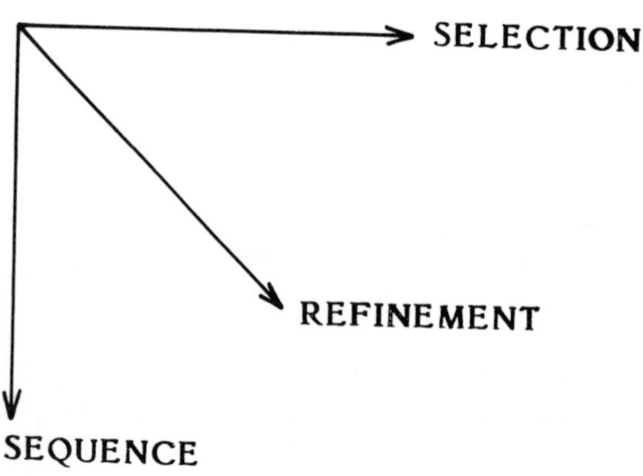
SELECTION
REFINEMENT
SEQUENCE

FLOWCHART CONVENTIONS

The earlier sequence given for processing a dish through the WASH process applies only for the processing of "one" dish. How can we indicate the processing of dishes one after another repetitively in sequence? For this purpose, we introduce a special conditional **repetitive sequence** structure that says **while predicate, do this sequence.** The predicate in our case is simply stated as indicated in the following flowchart.

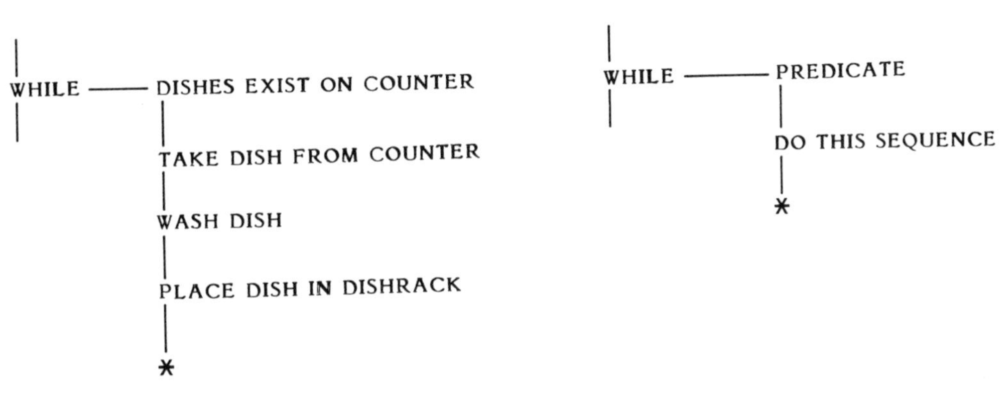

NOTE: * denotes the termination point of a repetitive sequence

A REPETITIVE SEQUENCE

Observe that the use of a special repetition symbol (*) indicates the termination point of a repetitive sequence.

The structures given thus far hopefully have given the reader some idea of the basic nature of process logic and programs at least in the informal context of our dish processing system. Let us now consider being somewhat more precise in describing the structure of process logic as is required in the computer system environment. In studying the following flowchart for the WASH process, the reader should review the earlier conventions and examples.

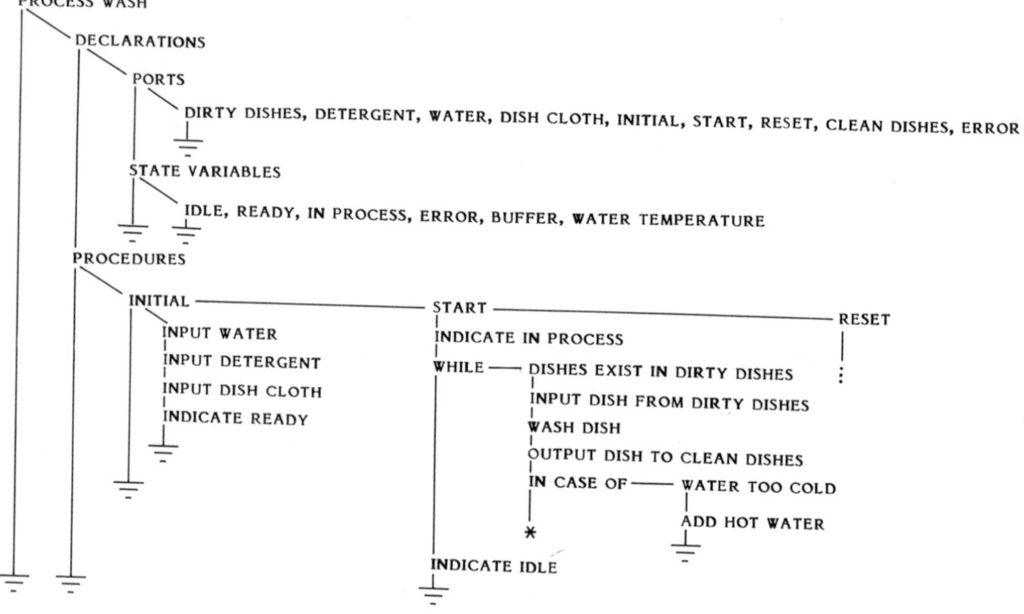

FLOWCHART OF PROCESS LOGIC

The process logic description is split into two parts. Firstly, **declarations** (i.e. enumeration) of all of the ports and state variables of the process. Secondly, **procedures** which are designed to execute the process logic. The procedures are started by control functions (i.e. signals) which call for the execution of the logic associated with the corresponding procedure. Note that the points of some of the state transitions are indicated in this partial flowchart. The treatment of potential errors in processing and the RESET procedure have not been described as their treatment is too involved for this introductory book.

The concepts illustrated in this chapter represent the backbone of computing technology and your mastery of them will enable you to proceed in studying the details of the field, if this is your goal, or, as a layreader, to appreciate the properties of logic and the programming process.

Summary

In summary, the changes of state that a process (machine) goes through during execution are called **state transitions** and a **state transition diagram** is a convenient pictorial representation of the possible changes of state and the reasons for each transition. Processes (machines) always have a limited "finite" number of states and are therefore referred to as **finite state machines.** In the computer system environment, the state of a process is represented in its **local storage** by **state indicators** which along with other local process objects are called the **state variables** of the process. The logic of a process is a plan for execution and the basic concepts of **sequence, selection, and refinement** along with **repetitive sequence** are the essential concepts for constructing a **program** which is synonymously referred to as an **algorithm. Flowcharts** provide a means of graphically representing the logic of a program. A program must be stated more concretely in the computer system environment and we have considered, in this chapter, a flowchart form in which **declarations** were made for the ports and state variables of a process and **procedures** were specified to correspond to control and error functions of process execution.

The author would like to thank Rob Witty of the Rutherford Laboratories, Oxfordshire, England for his pioneering work in developing the flowcharting conventions called "Dimensional Flowcharting," a variation of which has been introduced in this chapter.

Word List

Readers should verify their knowledge of the following terms (including analogies noted in parenthesis) by referring to the previous examples and solving the problems.

state transitions

finite state machine

state indicators

sequence

refinement

flowcharts (flowdiagrams)

declarations

state transition diagram

local storage

state variables

selection

program (algorithm)

repetitive sequence

procedures

Problems

1. Using the concepts applied in this chapter to the WASH process, build corresponding solutions for the DRY process as follows:

a). Based upon the machine like model of the DRY process from the previous chapter, draw a state transition diagram.

b). Draw an abstract model which shows the state variables of the process.

c). Construct a complete process description with declarations and procedures for the DRY process.

2. Construct a state transition diagram for your simplified coffee dispensing automat from the previous chapter. Further, create an abstract model which shows the state variables and create a complete process description which includes the required declarations and procedures.

Chapter 6
THE DATA PROCESSED BY COMPUTER SYSTEMS

In our real life analogy of the dish processing system, we illustrated the processing of objects "dishes"; however, we were able to consider many important analogous computer system related concepts. In the current chapter, we shall make the transition from these everyday objects with which we are accustomed to the objects (data) processed in the computer system environment.

The majority of computer system users today experience **human/machine communication** with a computer via a **terminal** which is connected to the computer system. We can view this connection as follows:

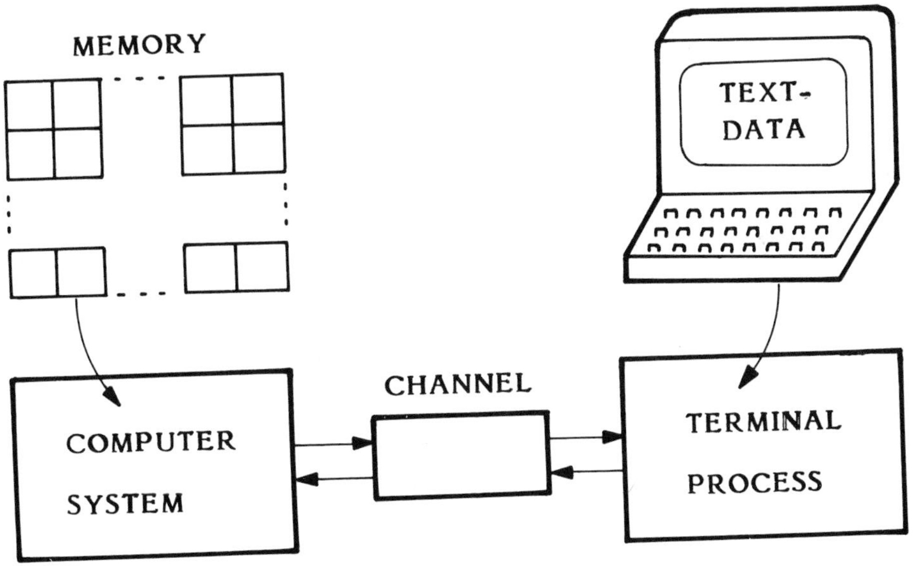

TERMINAL CONNECTION TO A COMPUTER SYSTEM

The terminal consists of a **terminal keyboard** and a **terminal screen.** The keyboard, in addition to providing the conventional typewriter keys, has some special keys used in the human/machine communication. The screen looks quite like an ordinary television screen.

The depression of keys at the terminal causes data to be transmitted over a channel to the computer system. The data received at the computer is placed into a **memory** owned by a memory storage process. The data is processed and the computer sends back data to the terminal screen. This data becomes "information" only when interpreted by human users in the context of their work. Note that a British synonym for the memory component of a computer system is a **store.**

For our purposes, in this chapter, we shall consider the computer system as a **"black box".** That is, a box (machine in our earlier discussions) that performs the required processing activities in some manner, the details of which are not of importance for the users. The particulars of the black box, including the detailed properties of the memory (store) component, will be discussed in the following chapter. The reader should note the use of "duplex" (two way communication) over the channel connecting the terminal to the computer system. Duplex and "half-duplex" transmission, as discussed in chapter 3, are the primary methods of communication between terminals and computer systems.

In this chapter, we shall study the "encoding" of the data that is processed by computer systems without studying the details of how the encoded data is processed. Basically, we can differentiate between two different types of data that are processed; namely, numbers and symbols. **Numbers** are those data objects upon which the computer system can apply arithmetic operations (addition, subtraction, multiplication and division) while **symbols** are non-numeric data which include the letters of the alphabet and other special symbols that can be typed in at the terminal keyboard and displayed on the terminal screen. Both forms of data are capable of being stored in the memory (store) which, amongst other usages, holds data while it is waiting to be processed. This is analogous to storages as introduced in chapter 3; for example, the counter or dishrack which held objects that were awaiting processing.

The numbers and symbols dealt with by users at the terminal are "human oriented" so that the user can make information interpretations; whereas, the computer system uses a highly "encoded" representation of numbers and symbols. We call the representations of data close to the user **external data representations** and those that are utilized in the memory (store) and processing within the computer system (black box) **internal data representations.**

Let us now proceed to consider these two data forms (numbers and symbols) of the computer system environment.

Numbers

In our real life analogy of the dish processing system, we processed objects "dishes" that were specified "declared" in the form of an alphabet of dishes. We human beings as processors of arithmetic calculations are trained to recognize and process arithmetic data according to the alphabet of **decimal digits** as follows:

ALPHABET OF DECIMAL DIGITS $\{0,1,2,3,4,5,6,7,8,9\}$

The alphabet here, as the alphabet of our dish processing system, enumerates the legitimate objects (data) that can be processed. Computer systems as processors of numerical data can only process data according to a very restricted alphabet; namely, the alphabet of **binary digits** which is as follows:

ALPHABET OF BINARY DIGITS $\{0,1\}$

Notice that this alphabet consists of only two members; namely the binary digits 0 and 1. The difference between these two alphabets is that they are constructed in conjunction with different **number bases.** In the alphabet of decimal numbers, we assume the use of the **decimal number system** base (10) and the decimal digits can have the value 0,1,2,3,4,5,6,7,8 and 9. In the alphabet of binary numbers, we assume the use of the **binary number system** base (2) with only the binary digits 0 and 1.

We may now ask the question: How are numbers of the binary number system made equivalent to the numbers from the decimal number system and therefore recognizable to we human processors that have been trained to perform arithmetic with decimal digits? To prove this equivalence let us consider the following examples.

We learn at an early age that the construction of decimal numbers is based upon the positions of the digits of the number as follows:

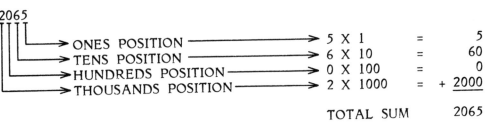

THE DECIMAL NUMBER 2065	IS EQUIVALENT TO		
ONES POSITION	5 X 1	=	5
TENS POSITION	6 X 10	=	60
HUNDREDS POSITION	0 X 100	=	0
THOUSANDS POSITION	2 X 1000	=	+ 2000
	TOTAL SUM		2065

CONSTRUCTION OF A DECIMAL NUMBER

Each digit position is multiplied by the value of the position in the decimal number base (1, 10, 100, 1000, etc.) and the number is then the sum of all of these results. We can observe that the decimal number base (10) is utilized since the value of each position is obtained by multiplying the previous position value by 10 (i.e. 1, 1x10 = 10, 10x10 = 100, 100x10 = 1000, etc.).

The construction of a binary number follows exactly the same rules with the only difference being that we use the binary number base (2). Consequently, the value of the positions in a binary number increase by multiplying by 2 (i.e. 1, 1x2 = 2, 2x2 = 4, 4x2 = 8, etc.). The construction of a binary number is illustrated as follows:

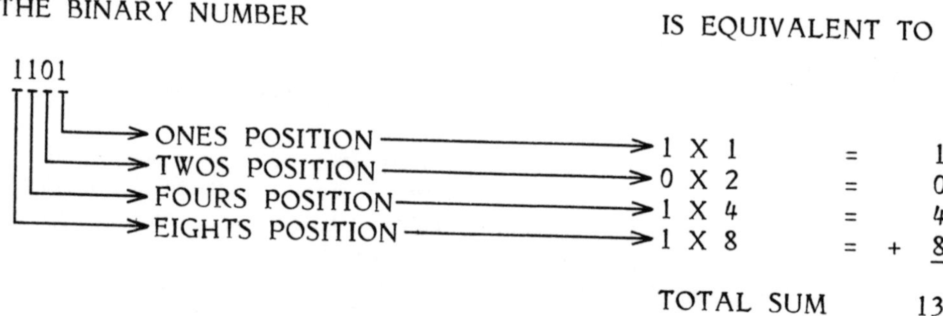

CONSTRUCTION OF A BINARY NUMBER

This binary number 1101, which is constructed only from members of the alphabet of binary digits, is equivalent to the decimal number 13. To further convince the reader that all binary numbers can be converted to and thus interpreted as equivalent decimal numbers, we shall consider the construction of a general process to convert binary numbers and a program (algorithm) for the process logic as follows:

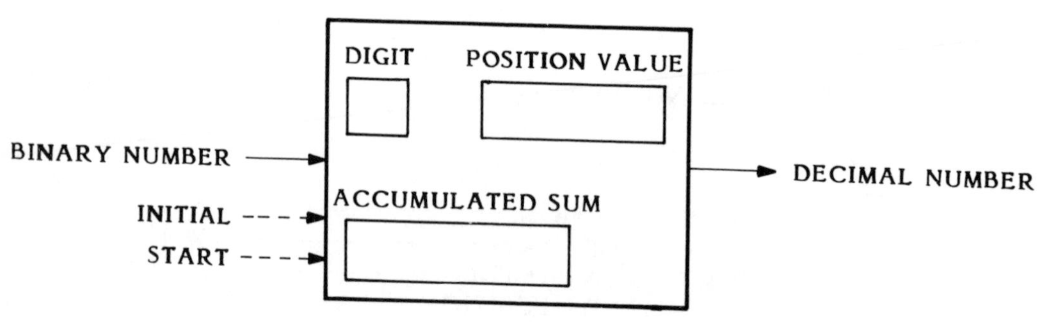

BINARY TO DECIMAL CONVERSION PROCESS

Note that three state variables are indicated within the local storage of the process. The flowchart for the process logic is as follows:

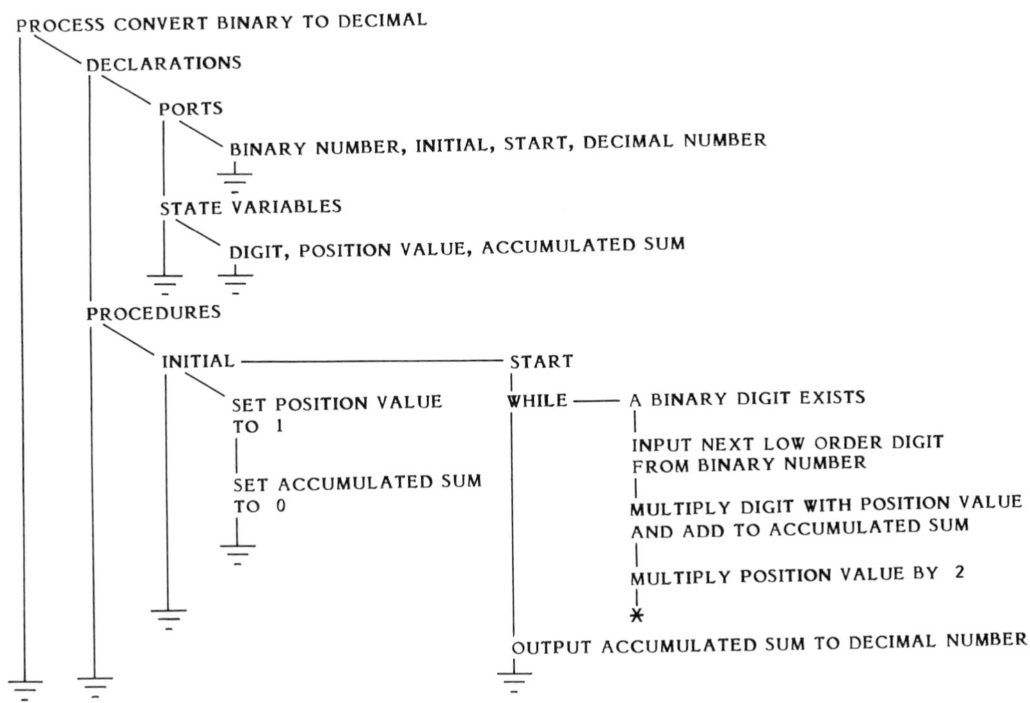
PROCESS CONVERT BINARY TO DECIMAL
DECLARATIONS
PORTS
BINARY NUMBER, INITIAL, START, DECIMAL NUMBER
STATE VARIABLES
DIGIT, POSITION VALUE, ACCUMULATED SUM
PROCEDURES
INITIAL
SET POSITION VALUE TO 1
SET ACCUMULATED SUM TO 0
START
WHILE
A BINARY DIGIT EXISTS
INPUT NEXT LOW ORDER DIGIT FROM BINARY NUMBER
MULTIPLY DIGIT WITH POSITION VALUE AND ADD TO ACCUMULATED SUM
MULTIPLY POSITION VALUE BY 2
*
OUTPUT ACCUMULATED SUM TO DECIMAL NUMBER

The state variables for POSITION VALUE and ACCUMULATED SUM must be initialized prior to the processing of the binary digits. The binary digits are processed from right to left. That is, the so-called "lower order digits" are processed (consumed) first. The reader should now, as a human processor for the process, use the algorithm to verify the conversion of the binary number 1101 to the decimal number 13. Further, try the following conversion, 100000010001, as well as constructing some of your own examples.

The binary number system is the basis of the numerical internal data representation utilized in computer system memories and in processing. However, we may ask the question: Why are binary numbers so advantageous and how are binary numbers represented in a computer system?

Representation of Binary Numbers

Binary digits which can only have the value 0 or 1 are represented via **electric signals** where two particular **voltage levels** of the signal indicate the binary value 0 or 1. Further, a changing of the voltage from the one voltage level to the other, over time, can change a binary 0 to a 1 or vice versa. In principle, any two voltage levels can be utilized for this purpose. In the following, we illustrate the use of 0 volts to represent a binary 0 and +2 volts to represent a binary 1.

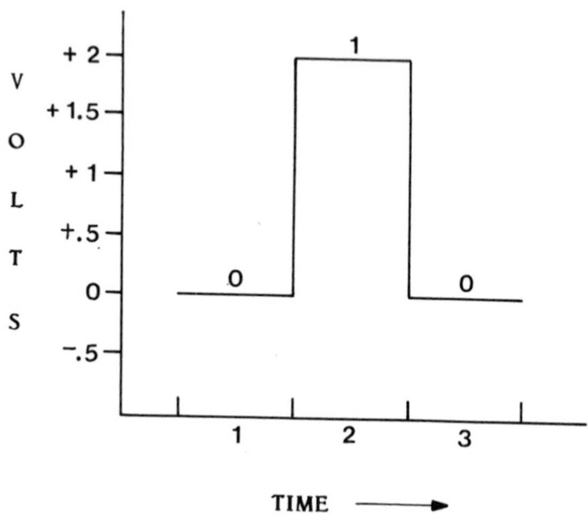

BINARY DIGIT REPRESENTATION BY VOLTAGE LEVEL

Notice that while the voltage is at level 0, the value of the signal is interpreted as binary 0, but when the voltage is raised to +2 volts, the value of the signal is interpreted as binary 1. Thus, in time frame one, it is 0, in time frame two, it is 1 and in time frame three, it is 0 again. This binary number 010 is equivalent to the decimal number 2. The reader should now construct a similar picture for the representation of the binary value 1101 consisting of four time frames.

The electronics of the computer system is equipped to make interpretations of the voltage levels within **tolerances.** That is, a voltage level near 0 volts is interpreted as a binary 0 and a voltage level near +2 volts is interpreted as a binary 1. This detail, however, is not essential to our further introductory understanding of computer systems.

Signals transported between the ports of various processes within a computer system use the channels as data carriers. It is possible, as illustrated above, to represent a binary number over successive time frames. Alternatively, we could utilize several simultaneous signals over a single time frame to represent a binary number. The transmission of binary numbers via a single signal over time is called **serial transmission;** whereas, when several signals are used simultaneously over a single time frame, the transmission is called **parallel transmission.** These transmission techniques are illustrated below.

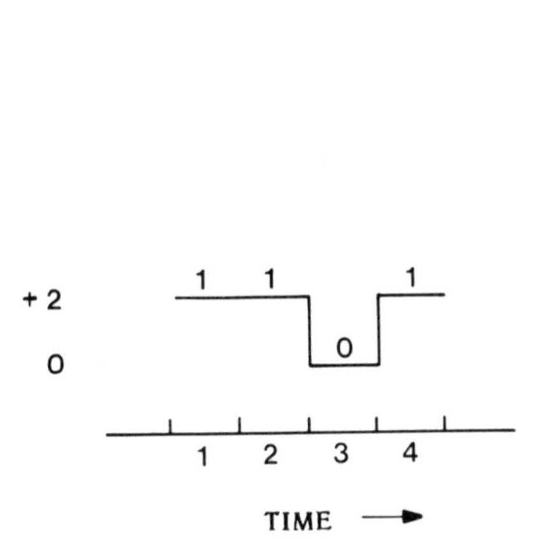

SERIAL TRANSMISSION

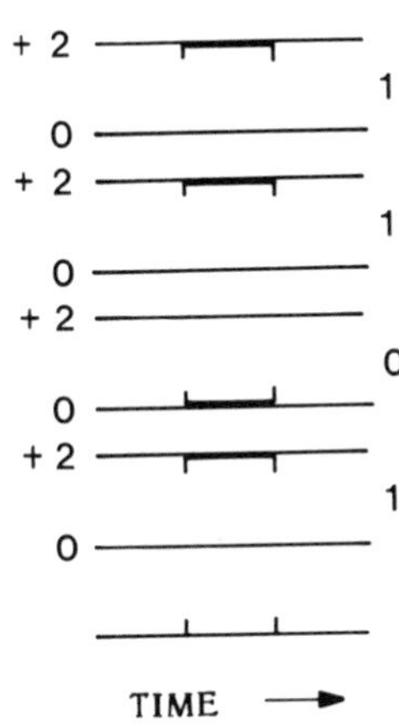

PARALLEL TRANSMISSION

The speed advantage of utilizing parallel signals (interpreted during a single time frame) as opposed to serial signals (interpreted over several time frames) should be obvious. Both serial and parallel transmission techniques are utilized in computer systems and further, their combination with the direction of transmission yields the following six possibilities.

simplex serial	simplex parallel
duplex serial	duplex parallel
half-duplex serial	half-duplex parallel

We may further ask the question: How many parallel signals or how many time periods are used in representing binary numbers? This maximum number of binary digits for binary number representation in computer systems is called the **precision** of the binary number. Real computer systems are normally designed to permit one or a limited number of different precisions but the precisions (maximum number of binary digits) are always limited "finite" for each system. Consequently, we cannot directly process as large a binary number as we desire. We are restricted by the "system constraint" of the available precision.

In the computer system environment, a binary signal is referred to as a **bit** and further, the precision of binary numbers permitted is normally expressed in terms of numbers of bits of precision instead of numbers of binary digits. The following is an enumeration of number of bits of precision commonly utilized in real computer systems and the resulting capacity of positive integer values permitted.

NUMBER OF BITS	RANGE OF INTEGER VALUES
4	0 to 15
8	0 to 255
16	0 to 65535
32	0 to 4294967295

It is also possible to represent negative integers and to represent non-integers (fractions) in computer systems; however, we shall not consider these representations in this introductory book.

Symbols

While computers are capable of performing arithmetic operations on binary numbers at remarkable electronic speeds (thousands, hundreds of thousands or even millions per second), we should not ignore their other important property in data processing; namely, the processing of non-numeric data (symbols). The symbols processed by the computer system are internal data representations of natural language alphabet characters and other symbols that we as users deal with as external data representations.

For every key stroke at the terminal keyboard, an internal data representation is created. The internal data representation is a fixed combination of bits for each unique symbol. We call this alphabet of internal representations the **character set** which specifies the encodings used to identify each unique external representation. There exist several standard character sets in use in the computer system environment. We select one such widely utilized standard code, namely the so-called ASCII alphabet (character set) to illustrate these properties. This alphabet appears on the following page.

Each symbol in the ASCII alphabet is represented by a fixed combination of seven (7) bits. Remembering our earlier discussions of the construction of binary numbers and precision, we can calculate that with 7 bits we can represent the values 0 to 127 decimal. Consequently, the ASCII alphabet is limited to 128 unique bit combinations; namely, 0000000 to 1111111 binary. To illustrate how to read this table, let us consider the internal encoding for the symbol B.

b6	b5	b4	b3	b2	b1	b0
1	0	0	0	0	1	0

<--- HIGH ORDER
LOW ORDER --->

ASCII REPRESENTATION OF THE SYMBOL B

BITS				b6 b5 b4	0 0 0	0 0 1	0 1 0	0 1 1	1 0 0	1 0 1	1 1 0	1 1 1
b3	b2	b1	b0									
0	0	0	0		NUL	DLE	SPACE	0	@	P	`	p
0	0	0	1		SOH	DC1	!	1	A	Q	a	q
0	0	1	0		STX	DC2	"	2	B	R	b	r
0	0	1	1		ETX	DC3	£	3	C	S	c	s
0	1	0	0		EOT	DC4	$	4	D	T	d	t
0	1	0	1		ENQ	NAK	%	5	E	U	e	u
0	1	1	0		ACK	SYN	&	6	F	V	f	v
0	1	1	1		BEL	ETB	'	7	G	W	g	w
1	0	0	0		BS	CAN	(	8	H	X	h	x
1	0	0	1		HT	EM	)	9	I	Y	i	y
1	0	1	0		LF	SUB	*	:	J	Z	j	z
1	0	1	1		VT	ESC	+	;	K	[	k	{
1	1	0	0		FF	FS	,	<	L	\	l	¦
1	1	0	1		CR	GS	-	=	M	]	m	}
1	1	1	0		SO	RS	.	>	N	^	n	~
1	1	1	1		SI	US	/	?	O	_	o	DEL

THE ASCII ALPHABET

The first three **high order bits** b6, b5 and b4 (100) are determined from the column in which B appears. The **low order bits** b3, b2, b1 and b0 (0010) are determined from the row in which B appears. From this table, we can identify symbols that can be created with a conventional typewriter and which are also available from the terminal keyboard. Other positions in the ASCII alphabet such as NUL, SOH, ..., DEL, etc. are not conventional typewriter keys. These members of the ASCII alphabet are called **control characters** and are normally used in controlling communications between the terminal and the computer system. Several of them are generated from the depression of special keys.

The collection of bits utilized to represent an ASCII character is frequently referred to as a **byte.** In reality, a byte is not normally seven (7) bits. Bytes are almost universally composed of eight (8) bits. An eighth bit precedes the seven bits of the ASCII representation; however, for our purposes, in this introductory book, we do not have to consider the function of this extra bit.

Let us now consider more precisely what happens in the human/machine communication in terms of the terminal process and computer system picture presented at the beginning of this chapter. Assume that we type the following text at the terminal keyboard:

Value is 13.

Further, after typing of the period (.), we depress the RETURN key (carriage return of a conventional typewriter). According to the ASCII alphabet, the following sequence of bits is generated in the terminal process and sent over the channel to the computer system.

	b6	b5	b4	b3	b2	b1	b0
V	1	0	1	0	1	1	0
a	1	1	0	0	0	0	1
l	1	1	0	1	1	0	0
u	1	1	1	0	1	0	1
e	1	1	0	0	1	0	1
SPACE	0	1	0	0	0	0	0
i	1	1	0	1	0	0	1
s	1	1	1	0	0	1	1
SPACE	0	1	0	0	0	0	0
1	0	1	1	0	0	0	1
3	0	1	1	0	0	1	1
.	0	1	0	1	1	1	0
CR	0	0	0	1	1	0	1

Note that a blank character is called a SPACE in the ASCII alphabet. The depressing of the RETURN key causes the CR (Carriage Return) encoding to be transmitted. The reader should examine several of these encodings by verifying their translation from the ASCII alphabet. This sequence is composed of 13 bytes; however, note that the eighth bit of each byte has not been illustrated.

The text of this **message** to the computer is stored in the memory of the computer system for further processing. As mentioned earlier, the manipulation of text (composed of symbols) is a very important property of computer systems that permits us to enter and modify (edit) texts. Further, programs are available to manipulate the text and format documents. These capabilities of computer systems are normally collectively referred to as **word processing systems.** In fact, this book was created via the use of a word processing system. We can view the word processing system which is composed of several processes as follows:

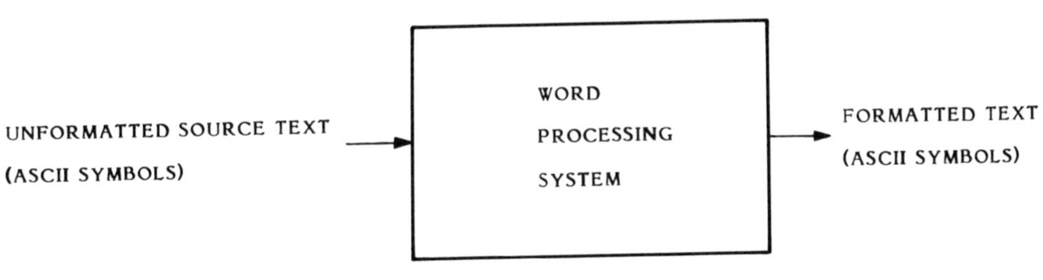

THE CREATION OF DOCUMENTS

The word processing system is, in reality, a suite of programs for the processes of the system. Unformatted source text as ASCII symbols are the data sent to the computer system and which are collected there in memories for further processing. When the word processing system processes the text, it creates formatted text that may then be displayed at the terminal or printed, as in the case of this book, on a printing device connected to the computer system. Thus, unformatted text is text entered without consideration to the final placement of the text in the document (formatted text) to be produced. The user can select the type of formats, titles, page numbering, section numbering, etc. that is required for the final document.

Another very important utilization of text is the entry of computer programs in their external form into the computer system. The programs entered are called **source programs;** however, these programs are not, at this point, in the proper internal format (representation) for interpretation by the computer system. They must be "translated" from the external source program representation into the appropriate internal representation called the **object program.** Consequently, the source program is data to a **translation system** which is composed of several processes as illustrated in the following picture:

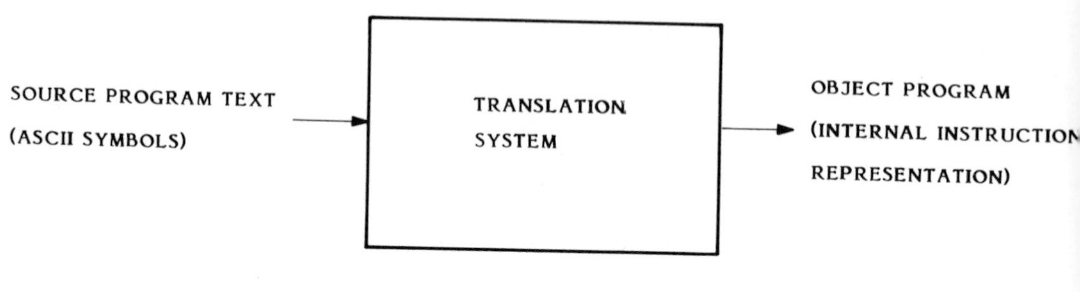

THE TRANSLATION OF PROGRAMS

Again, it is important to remember that the translation system is, in reality, a suite of programs for the processes of the system. Consequently, though it may seem strange at first, we use the programs of the translation system to translate other new programs. The details of the various **programming languages** utilized in the computer system environment are, of course, outside the scope of this introductory book. In any event, the flowchart normally represents an abstract description of the structure of a program from which the programmer makes a concrete description in some particular programming language. There exist so-called **low level languages** which are closely related to the detailed structure and operation of the computer system and so-called **higher level languages** in which case the programmer is freed from knowing the details of the particular computer system utilized. The names of several of these higher level languages such as FORTRAN, COBOL, PL/I, BASIC, ALGOL, APL, SIMULA, PASCAL and ADA, to name a few, may already be familiar to the reader. In succeeding chapters, we shall further discuss the utilization of both low level and high level languages.

Data Structures

An important aspect of the entry and processing of data is concerned with how the data is organized; that is, the **data structure.** Each individual data item, a number or a collection of related symbols, is referred to as a **scalar** value. We can frequently find motivations for organizing groups of related scalar values into regular structures which are quite logical and/or which provide for more efficient processing. Returning for a moment to our dish processing system analogy, there could be a motivation to process (wash and/or dry) all objects of the same type in sequence; for example, all cups. There may also be motivation to process sets of related dishes; for example, a cup, a saucer, a salad dish and a meat dish. These collections of objects are called **arrays** and **structures**, respectively, and can be visualized as follows:

AN ARRAY OF SCALAR ITEMS

STRUCTURES OF SCALAR ITEMS

The important thing to remember is that in an array, all elements are of the same basic type; whereas, structures are a collection (set) of related but different types of objects. A common synonym for the term structure in the computer system environment is **record.**

Let us now consider the motivation for some data structures that are organized conveniently for processing by computer systems and their human users. Firstly, let us consider an array as follows:

84 75 62 91 87 81

AN ARRAY OF EXAMINATION RESULTS

This array collects together examination results which are the same basic type of scalar value. We may, for example, have a program (algorithm) that goes through the array and accumulates the sum of all of the array elements; finally, it calculates the average grade of 80 (i.e. 480 divided by 6).

A structure (record) which can contain several different types of scalar objects is exemplified as follows:

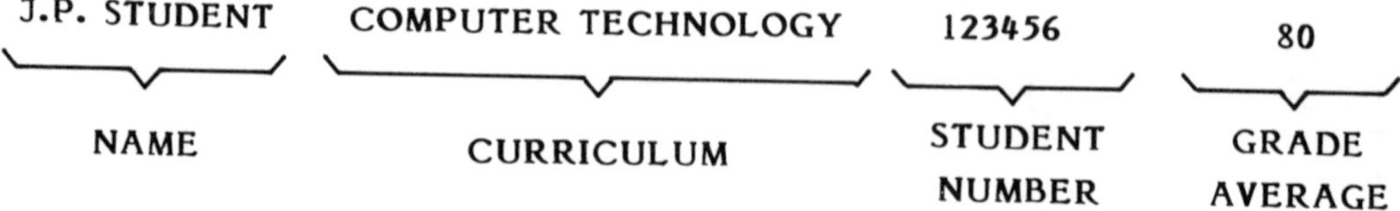

A STRUCTURE (RECORD) OF A STUDENT

The value of the structure (record) is the collection of individual scalar items given for the student, including his name. The identifications of various parts of the structure are referred to as **field names.** Thus, each individual value within the structure is referred to as a **field** of the structure. Messages sent to computer systems, processed by the computer system and received from the computer system can contain scalar values, arrays, structures (records) or combinations of these data structure types.

Summary

In summary, most users have their **human/machine communication** with computer systems via a **terminal** which is composed of a **terminal keyboard** and a **terminal screen.** From the user's viewpoint, the computer system can be thought of as a **black box** that contains a **memory (store)** which, amongst other uses, holds data while they are not being processed. The computer system is equipped to process two types of data; namely, **numbers** upon which arithmetic operations can be performed and **symbols** which are non-numeric data that can be typed in from the terminal keyboard and displayed on the terminal screen. Data representations which are human oriented are called **external data representations;** whereas, the representations used in storing data and in their processing are called **internal data representations.**

We human processors of arithmetic data are trained to deal with the **decimal digits** (0,1,..,9); whereas, computer systems are equipped to deal with **binary digits** (0,1). These two sets of numbers belong to two different **number bases;** namely, the **decimal number system** base (10) and the **binary number system** base (2). The advantage of using the binary number system in the computer system environment is that binary digits can be easily represented by **electric signals** where only two **voltage levels** are required; namely, one voltage level to represent binary 0 and another to represent binary 1. The electronics of the computer system is equipped to recognize these voltage levels within **tolerances.** When a single signal is used over several time frames to transmit a binary number, it is called **serial transmission,** in contrast to the use of **parallel transmission** where several signals are used simultaneously over a single time frame for binary number representation.

The maximum number of binary digits that are permitted in the processing operations of a computer system is called the **precision.** Further, the precision is normally expressed in terms of numbers of **bits** instead of binary digits. External symbol representations as seen by the user are converted to internal symbol representations according to an alphabet called the **character set.** The ASCII alphabet (character set) which is a seven (7) bit code was used as an example. Within a symbol encoding (or a binary number for that matter), the left most bits are called the **high order bits** and the right most bits are called the **low order bits.** In addition to containing representations for natural language alphabet symbols, the ASCII alphabet contains so-called **control characters** which are used in controlling communications between the terminal and the computer system. In real computer systems, ASCII characters are normally contained in groups of eight (8) bits and are called **bytes.**

Collections of symbols entered at the terminal and sent to the computer system and vice versa are called **messages.** The text of documents, letters, books, etc., can be entered as messages and collected in the computer system memories for further processing by a **word processing system** which produces the desired formatted text. Another important use of message texts as data is the communication of programs in their so-called **source program** format for translation into an internal (instruction) representation called the **object program** via a **translation system.** The programs are constructed according to the rules and conventions of a **programming language.** Programming languages that are closely related to the details of computer system structure and operation are called **low level languages;** whereas, **higher level languages** are used to free the programmer from being concerned with the details of the computer system.

Data to be processed by computer systems are frequently organized into **data structures.** A single value is referred to as a **scalar** value. Collections of the same types of scalar values are called **arrays** and collections of related scalar values of different types are called **structures (records).** The individual values of structures are identified by **field names** and are thus themselves referred to simply as **fields** of the structure.

Word List

Readers should verify their knowledge of the terminology and concepts presented in this first chapter related directly to the computer system environment by reviewing the examples and solving the problems.

human/machine communication	terminal
terminal keyboard	terminal screen
black box	memory (store)
numbers	symbols
internal data representations	external data representations
decimal digits	binary digits
number base	decimal number system
binary number system	electric signals
voltage level	tolerances
serial transmission	parallel transmission
precision	bit
character set	low order bits
high order bits	control characters
bytes	messages
word processing system	source program
object program	translation system
programming languages	low level languages
higher level languages	data structures
scalar	array
structure (record)	field names
field	

Problems

1. Show how the following decimal numbers are constructed according to the decimal number system base (10) by multiplication of digit values by the value of positions and the addition of these results.

    5, 32, 409, 5061, 88300, 265321

2. Show how the following binary numbers are constructed according to the binary number system base (2) by multiplication of binary digit values by the value of positions and the addition of these results.

    1, 10, 011, 101, 1001, 10101, 100000, 1111111

3. Create pictures of the electric signal representation of the binary numbers given in (2) with the required number of time frames. Use the voltage level 0 to represent a binary 0 and the voltage level +2 to represent a binary 1.

4. For each of the pictures created in (3) which represent "serial transmission" of binary numbers, create a corresponding picture which illustrates "parallel transmission" of the binary numbers by utilizing a signal for each binary digit.

5. What is the range of positive integer decimal values that can be represented as a binary number of 12, 24 and 36 bits of precision.

6. Show the translation of the following messages, composed of symbols according to the ASCII alphabet, by utilizing the ASCII character set table given in this chapter. Assume that each message is terminated by depression of the RETURN key.

    This is a sentence.

    LOAD 5, ALPHA

    A=B+1;

7. Create an array of seven (7) scalar values which contains the average daily temperature for the last calender week. Create a picture of a process (machine) which inputs these items and outputs the average temperature for the week (note: use INITIAL and START signals and identify and name required state variables). Construct a dimensional flowchart of the logic of the process. Follow the process logic by interpreting it step by step to verify that the logic works for the given input data (temperature array).

8. Construct a structure (record) which contains the following information about yourself: Name, address, age, height, weight, eye color. Label each field with the corresponding field name.

Chapter 7
THE COMPUTER AS A SYSTEM OF COOPERATING PROCESSES

In chapters 2 to 5, we have introduced the concepts of processes, systems, data flow, control and process logic (programming) with analogies to real life equivalents. In the previous chapter, we treated the computer system as a "black box" while studying the characteristics of external and internal data representations. Now it is time to utilize this knowledge to study the inner structure of computer systems. A general structure for the main processes in a computer system is as follows:

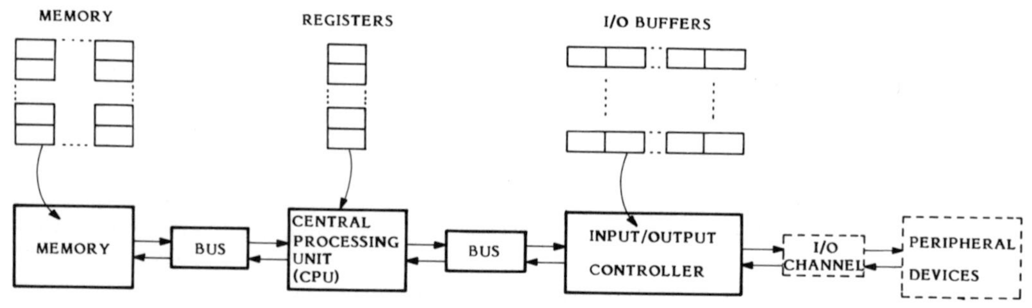

THE COOPERATING PROCESSES OF A COMPUTER SYSTEM

The structured flowcharting conventions introduced in chapter 5 provide us with a general tool for illustrating the structure of the processes in a computer system which is, as we can observe, a "system of cooperating processes" as follows:

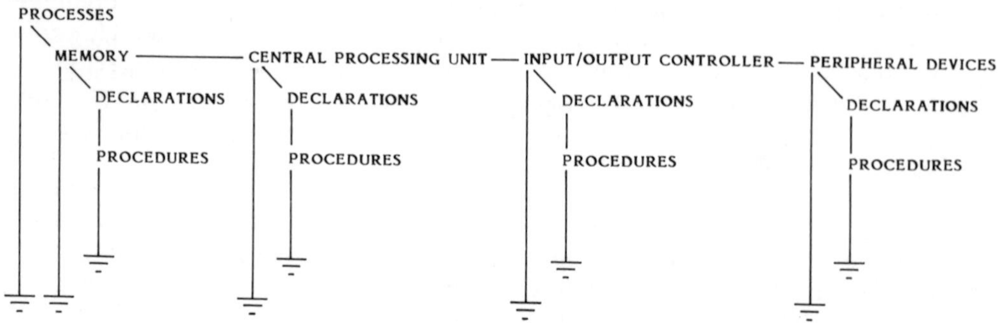

In the flowchart form, we show the skeleton structure of the processes, each with their own process logic (program) that corresponds to the illustrated processes. The collection of cooperating processes in a real computer system is called the computer **configuration.** The memory, central processing unit and Input/Output controller processes correspond to the "black box" of the previous chapter.

Note that processes of the system communicate via "channels" with "duplex transmission" (transmission in both directions). Some of the transmission channels within a computer system are referred to as **buses** and the term **highway** is a British synonym for this component. The following brief description of each of the processes indicated will be followed later in the chapter by more detailed explanations.

Memory or the British synonym **store** (as mentioned in the previous chapter) is a "storage process" that has two functions. Firstly, it holds data while it is not being processed by the central processing unit. Secondly, the memory contains the **instructions** of programs which the central processing unit follows in executing its processing functions.

Central Processing Unit which is normally abbreviated to CPU, is the main computational and symbol manipulating process (machine) of the computer system. It is endowed with capabilities for manipulating symbols and performing arithmetic operations (addition, subtraction, multiplication and division); further, it is capable of making decisions and following alternative paths of program actions. Most important, the CPU is a stupid, but obedient, "interpreter" of programs that are contained in the memory. The program "instructions" tell the CPU exactly and precisely which processing operations to perform.

Input/Output Controller through cooperation with the central processing unit maintains contact with so-called "peripheral devices" which are the producers and consumers of data, including programs processed by the computer system.

Peripheral Devices is the denotation given to a wide category of devices that can be connected to the computer system; thus, we utilize dotted connections here to indicate that several **I/O channels** and several peripheral devices can be connected to the Input/Output controller. Some of the devices are dedicated to storing large quantities of data and programs. Other peripheral equipment may be devices used to take measurements (for example, temperature from a real physical process that the computer system is controlling) or devices that activate "signal" the execution of physical procedures in the process. Still others are terminals (as described in the previous chapter) and printer devices used in "human/machine communication" with the computer system. The properties of several peripheral devices will be described in the next chapter.

Each of the processes may be thought of as a "finite state machine" with its own local storage containing state variables as described in the earlier chapters. We have illustrated here the processes of the computer system, but remember, as we learned already in chapter 2, **a process can only be carried out "executed" when a processor is applied.** What then are the processors? The processors of these processes are what is referred to collectively as the **computer hardware.** The hardware represents the electronic components which are equipped to process the binary electric signals as described in the previous chapter. Through programs, contained in the computer memory, we direct the various cooperating processes of the computer system to realize the processes of our computer system applications. These programs contained in the memory or contained in peripheral storage devices are collectively referred to as the **computer software.**

The Structure of Registers, Memories and Buffers

The **registers** of the central processing unit (CPU), the memory (store) of the memory process and the **I/O buffers** of the Input/Output controller are all local storages owned by the respective processes and utilized in accomplishing the processing activities of the process. All of them hold data (numbers or symbols) or program instructions in their internal representation. The difference between these local storages is **not** in structure, but is in size (capacity) and their so-called **access time.** The registers of the CPU which are normally quite limited in number also have the fastest access time. The memory which can contain a reasonably large quantity of data or instructions is normally somewhat slower. The number of I/O buffers and their access times varies quite widely amongst computer systems.

The registers of the CPU are storage elements capable of holding data values of a maximum number of bits of precision. The precision varies from computer system to computer system, but sizes of 8, 12, 16, 24, 32, 36, 48 and 64 bits are most common. Further, each register in the CPU has a unique **register address** as illustrated in the following picture.

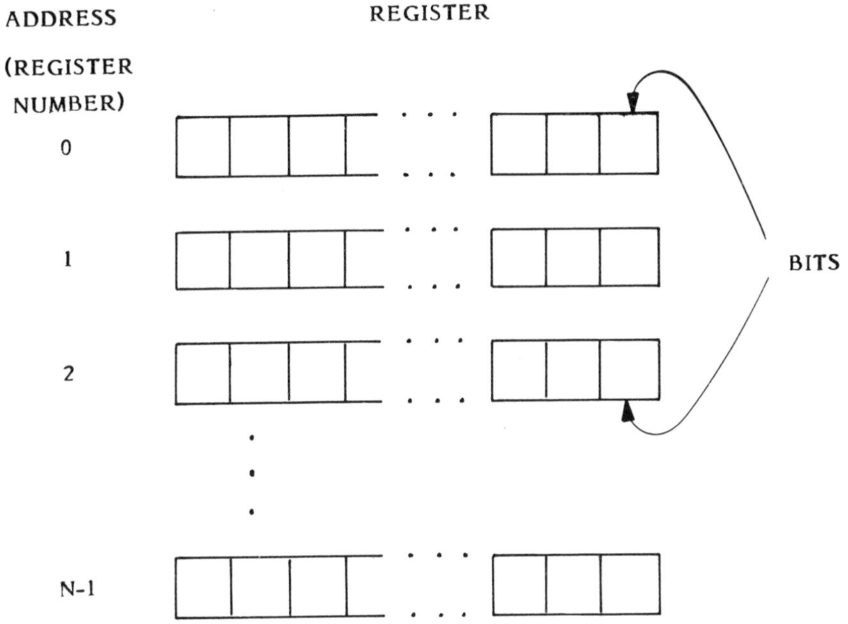

ADDRESS (REGISTER NUMBER) | REGISTER

0

1

2

N-1

BITS

ADDRESSABLE REGISTERS OF THE CPU

We can think of the registers as a pigeon-hole rack with labels (addresses) for each pigeon-hole. Imagine a postal clerk sorting (processing) a pile of mail and placing them in the pigeon-holes based upon addresses on the letters. Likewise, instructions processed by the CPU specify register addresses to identify the registers to be accessed and utilized in CPU processing operations.

The number of registers in the CPU varies from computer system to computer system but quantities of 2, 4, 8, 16, 32, 64, 128 or 256 are common. Computer systems with more than 256 CPU registers exist but are in the minority. The reader can observe that the registers hold representations of binary numbers. Further, these registers are "inputs" to arithmetic calculations (addition, subtraction, multiplication and division). Note that register addresses begin with zero (0) and proceed up to N-1. N in this case is the total number of registers.

The memory (store) of the memory process is, like registers, a storage element capable of holding data values of a maximum number of bits of precision. The precision of these storage elements, referred to as **memory cells,** synonymously **memory words,** normally corresponds to the precision of the registers in the CPU. Like the registers of the CPU, each memory cell has a unique **memory address** as illustrated in the following picture.

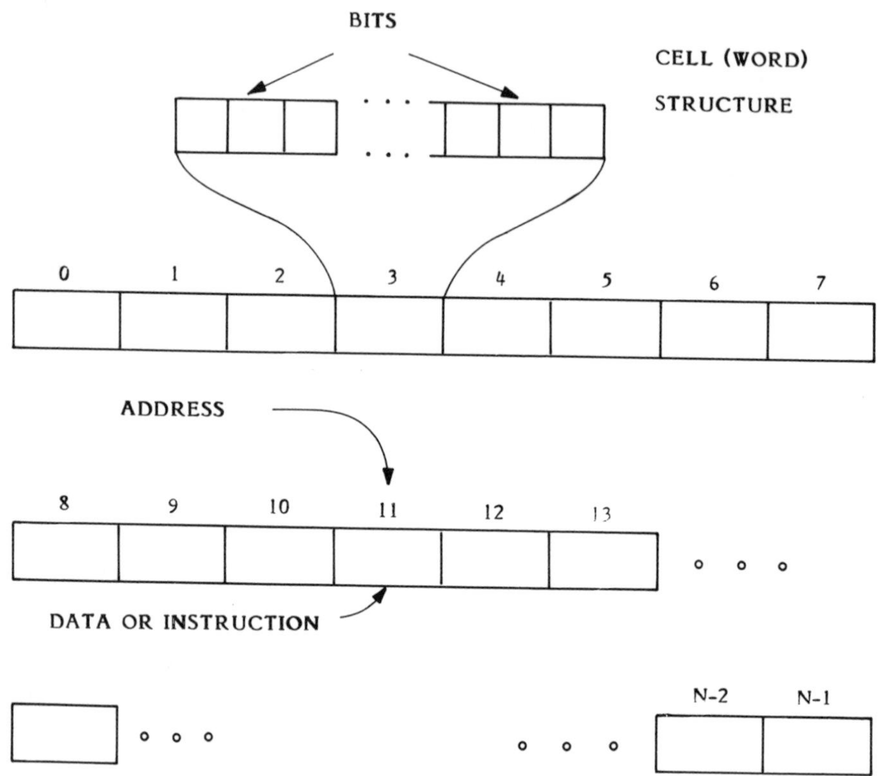

A RANDOM ACCESS MEMORY (RAM)

Again think of this structure simply as a larger pigeon-hole rack with more addresses. Instructions processed by the CPU, in addition to defining the addresses of registers (where required), specify the address of memory cells to be utilized in processing (where required). Note: No processing takes place in the memory process itself since it is simply a storage process. Further, observe that as with register addresses, the first memory address is zero (0) and the highest address is N-1, where N is the total number of memory cells (words).

The memory in the memory process is usually referred to as a **Random Access Memory** (RAM) since memory cells (words) do not have to be accessed in any particular order. A memory cell can be utilized to contain data (numbers or symbols) or instructions to be processed by the CPU, but **not** both at the same time. Data structures of the array type and the structure type, as introduced in the previous chapter, can occupy several consecutive memory cells.

The capacity of the memories utilized varies from computer system to computer system but it can be as few as several hundred memory cells up to several million memory cells.

Each I/O buffer utilized in the I/O controller is normally composed of a fixed number of cells. These buffers are temporary holding places for collecting messages in transmission to or from the CPU. The CPU places the messages, possibly containing data structures, into or takes the messages from the memory. The buffers here like the buffers discussed in the "asynchronous control" concepts of chapter 4, permit the operation of the CPU-memory complex to proceed largely independent of the speed of operation of the peripheral devices connected to the computer system. When sufficiently large quantities of data are to be transmitted to the memory, an "interrupt" signal is given from the I/O controller to the CPU. To transmit data from the memory, the CPU "initiates" the transfer by interrupting the I/O controller. Note the CPU-memory complex performs operations at a far greater speed then the fastest of peripheral devices.

Buses, I/O Channels, Data Transmission and Control Signals

The transmission of **both** data signals and control signals between the cooperating processes of the computer system is made over buses (for the central processes) and I/O channels (for the peripheral processes). A general structure for these transmission media is as follows:

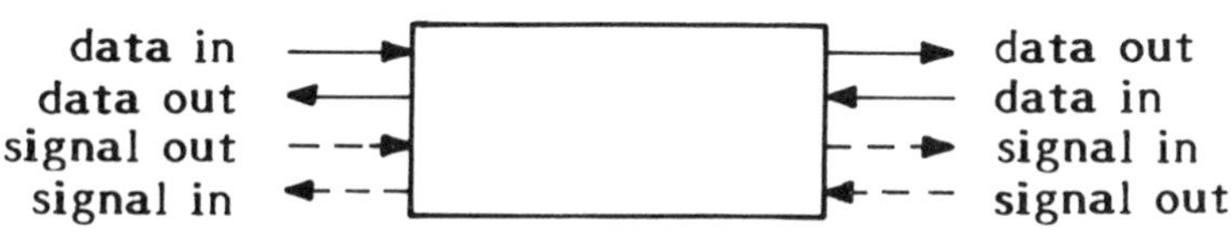

BUS (HIGHWAY) AND I/O CHANNEL

TRANSMISSION OF DATA AND CONTROL SIGNALS

In the case of "serial transmission" of binary data signals, as described in the previous chapter, single signal lines (connections) are utilized. However, for "parallel transmission," several data signals are utilized. Parallel transmission is almost always used in the central processes for buses (highways); whereas, parallel and serial I/O channels are utilized based upon the requirements for speed of transfer to and from specific peripheral devices.

Process Interfaces

Let us now proceed by considering some further details of the central cooperating processes. Namely, we shall consider how control signals are utilized to inform neighboring processes about what is to be done and when it is to be done. We shall consider this in two stages; firstly, the connections of the CPU-memory complex and then the CPU-I/O controller. The connections between the CPU and memory processes are illustrated as follows:

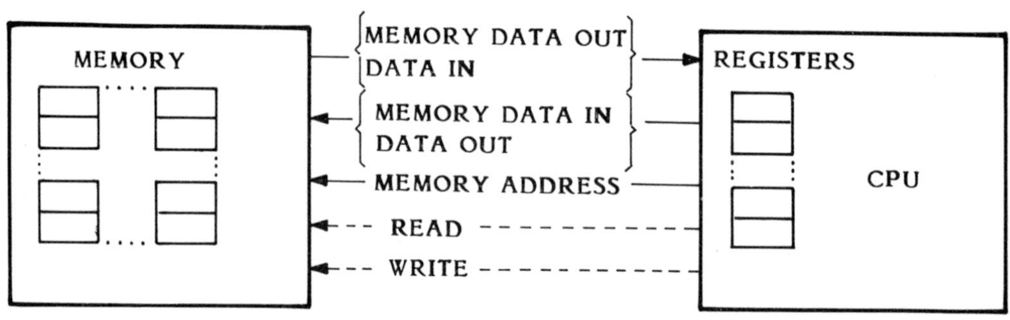

THE CPU MEMORY COMPLEX

Notice that we show the data and control signals that belong to the bus (highway) that connects these two processes. The central processing unit which owns the fastest resources (the registers) and has computational and decision making capability is the controlling process and thus tells the memory process what to do and when to do it. The connections between any two processes in a computer system is called the **interface** between the processes. Further, the procedures (rules) to be followed in sending and receiving control signals and data are called the **protocol.** Protocol in this context is analogous to the use of the term protocol in governmental diplomatic circles which also specify formal procedures (rules) of conduct.

The data and control signals are given **signal names** and notice that in the case of two of the signals, two names are given; namely, the appropriate name as seen from both sides of the interface. We shall now consider the protocols used by the CPU in "reading from" and "writing to" a memory cell (word). The read protocol sequence is as follows:

PLACE DESIRED ADDRESS ON THE MEMORY ADDRESS SIGNALS

ISSUE THE READ SIGNAL

RECEIVE DATA OR INSTRUCTIONS OVER THE DATA IN SIGNALS

MEMORY READ PROTOCOL

The memory process finds the memory cell (word) corresponding to the memory address and sends the **memory cell contents** to the CPU. **Important:** the contents of the memory cell remain unchanged as a result of this operation. Thus the reading from this random access memory (RAM) is called a **non-destructive read.** This is obviously different from when we take (read) an object (dish) from a dishrack storage, in which case the dish disappears from the dishrack.

The protocol for the memory write is as follows:

PLACE DESIRED ADDRESS ON THE MEMORY ADDRESS SIGNALS

PLACE DATA OR INSTRUCTIONS ON THE DATA OUT SIGNALS

ISSUE THE WRITE SIGNAL

MEMORY WRITE PROTOCOL

The memory process finds the memory cell corresponding to the memory address given and then replaces the current contents of the addressed cell with the value of the new data or instructions. The writing into a memory cell is called a **destructive write.** After writing, the previous contents of the cell are permanently destroyed.

Let us now turn our attention to the interface and protocol used between the CPU and the I/O controller which is illustrated as follows:

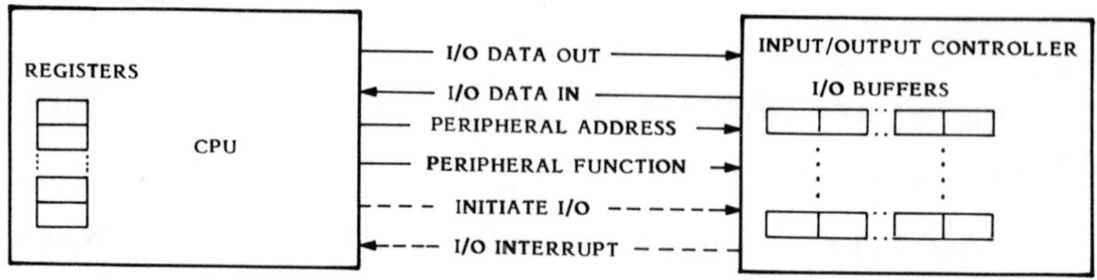

THE CPU-I/O CONTROLLER INTERFACE

The question of who is in control between these two processes is slightly more complicated. In principle, the CPU, following directions of the program, controls the transmission of data to and from peripheral devices. However, a peripheral device can, via the I/O controller, cause an "interrupt" (like the baby crying in chapter 2) and thus gain the attention of the CPU indicating that it is ready to or wants to perform input and/or output transfers. A good example of such an interrupt is the signal sent when we turn on our terminal.

In addition to being able to send data (write) to and receive data (read) from peripherals, the CPU can issue other so-called **I/O control functions.** These functions are particular to each peripheral category. We shall not attempt to illustrate all possible protocols used in this interface, but will instead consider simply the reading and writing functions.

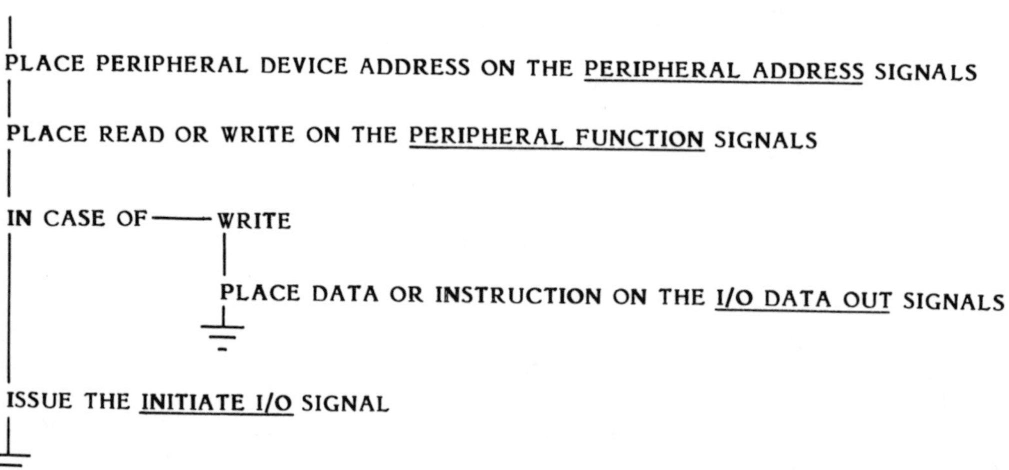

INPUT/OUTPUT FUNCTION PROTOCOL

In the case of reading from a peripheral device, data or instructions coming from the peripheral device are first collected in buffers and then transmitted over to the CPU which further sends them to the memory. When writing to a peripheral device, data or instructions are taken from the memory by the CPU which then sends them to the I/O controller. The I/O controller uses the buffers as an intermediary before transmitting to the peripheral device. Remember, as mentioned earlier in this chapter, the buffers permit the use of asynchronous (speed independent) control of the peripheral devices so that they can work at their own pace.

The CPU, Instructions and Programs

As mentioned several times in this book, a computer system is a stupid but obedient and extremely fast follower of our instructions. The instructions are given to the computer in the form of a program which is simply a well ordered collection of instructions in the same sense that a recipe contains well ordered instructions for cooking your favorite dish. Programs control computer operations and **people** write programs. Consequently, people endow the computer with any small level of "intelligence" which may be attributed to computer systems.

The well ordered instructions of the computer system are contained in memory cells and each "instruction" is constituted as a configuration of bits. The instruction always has an **operation code field** which identifies the instruction type. This bit pattern is fixed for each of the instruction types recognized for interpretation by the computer system's interpreting mechanism, namely, the central processing unit. The entire collection of these recognizable instructions is called the computer's **instruction repertoire.** The repertoire varies from computer system to computer system; however, a repertoire can contain as few as 10 to 20 unique instructions up to several hundred unique instructions. Many instructions also require the specification of so-called **operand fields** which identify objects (data or instructions) that are to be involved in instruction execution (for example, involved in arithmetic operations). The general format of an instruction is as follows:

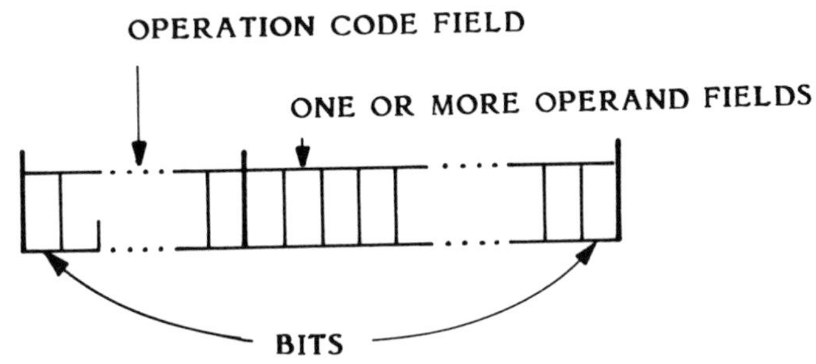

INSTRUCTION FORMAT

The exact number of bits occupied by the operation code field and operand fields varies from computer system to computer system; however, within any particular computer system, the number of bits is precisely and rigidly prescribed. In some computer systems, an instruction is always exactly the size of one memory cell (word); whereas, in other computer systems, especially where several operand fields may be given, instructions may require several consecutive memory cells.

The instructions recognized by the computer system are designed to control the internal operation of the computer and are divided into categories which relate to functions of the cooperating processes described earlier. These categories, typically found in a large class of computer systems, are as follows:

- Input/Output Instructions
- Data Conversion Instructions
- Register Loading and Storing Instructions
- Arithmetic Instructions
- Symbol Manipulation Instructions
- Control Instructions

The central processing unit, as an interpreter of these instructions, carries out the processing operations on data. The internal state variables of the CPU and its input and output ports are illustrated as follows:

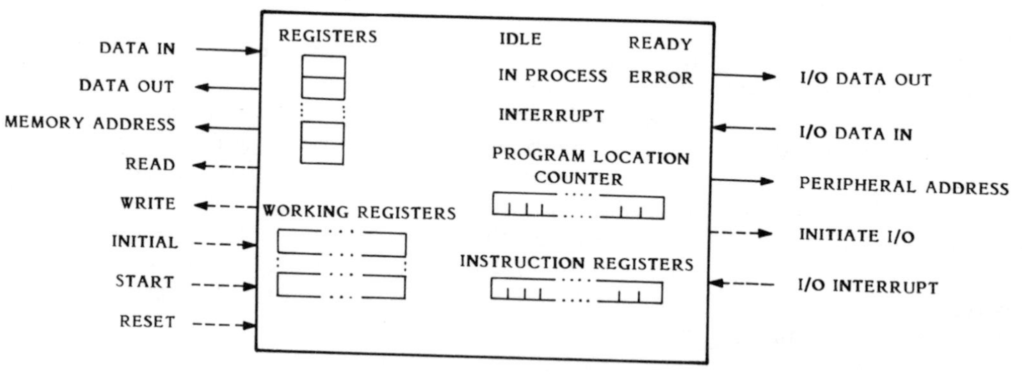

THE CENTRAL PROCESSING UNIT

Here we can identify four state indicators; namely IDLE, READY, IN PROCESS and ERROR which correspond to our earlier example of the WASH process as a finite state machine. We add an INTERRUPT state indicator which is used to indicate that the CPU has been interrupted by an I/O interrupt and has temporarily diverted its attention to servicing this interrupt. These state indicators define the general states that the CPU can be in at every moment of time, and we can therefore consider the following "state transition diagram," which contains the same states as our earlier description of the WASH process with the only addition being the INTERRUPT state.

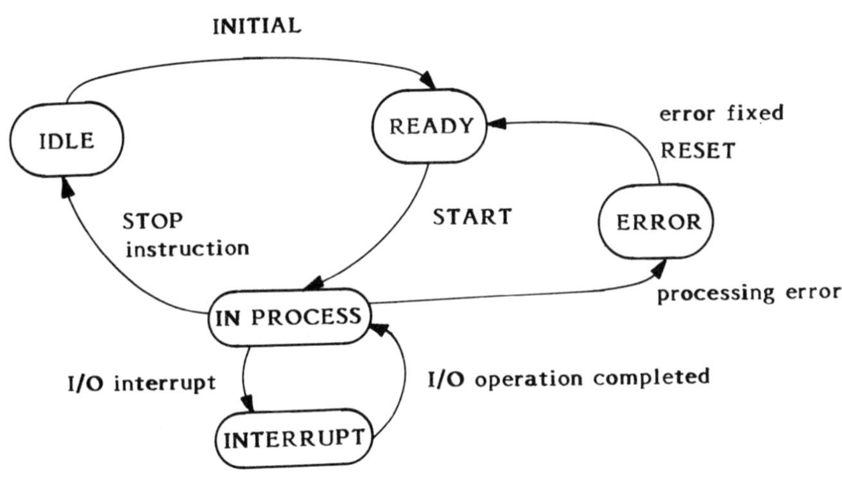

CPU STATE TRANSITION DIAGRAM

In addition to the addressable REGISTERS of the CPU, there normally exist several so-called WORKING REGISTERS that are purely local storage of the CPU and are utilized in assisting in performing its operations, including its role as intermediary in I/O transfers. The remaining state variables, namely, the PROGRAM LOCATION COUNTER and the INSTRUCTION REGISTER are the main state objects used for processing the instructions which are "fetched" (read) from the memory process. The PROGRAM LOCATION COUNTER identifies the address of the "next instruction" to be fetched from the memory for execution. The INSTRUCTION REGISTER is a buffer that holds the "current instruction" under execution. The PROGRAM LOCATION COUNTER is incremented by the size of the instruction being executed so that its fetch of the "next instruction" is made from the beginning address of the instruction in the memory. The size of an instruction is the number of memory cells (words) that the instruction occupies in the memory.

The execution of an instruction by the CPU is a two step cycle, namely, "fetch instruction" and then "execute instruction." The logic of this part of the CPU process, as well as the general structure of the CPU process logic, is given in the flowchart on the following page.

The INITIAL, START and RESET signals viewed earlier in the abstract picture of the CPU can, in fact, be push buttons on the physical CPU and the states may well be indicated by lights. In initializing the system, the REGISTERS are set to zero values; next, a startup program is "loaded" into the memory from a storage type peripheral device and placed starting at memory location (0). There exist several detailed operations which are not further refined in this loading sequence. Initialization continues by clearing the PROGRAM LOCATION COUNTER to zero (0) and indicating the READY state.

When the START signal is received, the IN PROCESS state is entered and the instruction fetch, instruction execution cycle is started. Note the use of a "repetitive sequence" with the predicate WHILE --- IN PROCESS, to show that the cycle is repeated, and the use of "refinement" to illuminate the activities involved in the two parts of this cycle. The process logic for the CPU process includes, for instruction execution, the predicate selection of the operation to be performed via the instruction category. The category can be determined by examining a subset of the bits of the earlier named operation code field. The details of instruction execution logic are not given here and are not essential for our basic understanding of computer systems. The STOP instruction places the CPU into the IDLE state as indicated earlier in the state transition diagram.

The details of the handling of error conditions which vary from computer system to computer system will not be considered. Notice the INTERRUPT procedure which is activated due to an I/O INTERRUPT. In this procedure, the INTERRUPT state is entered; after the interrupt is serviced, the CPU is returned to the IN PROCESS state.

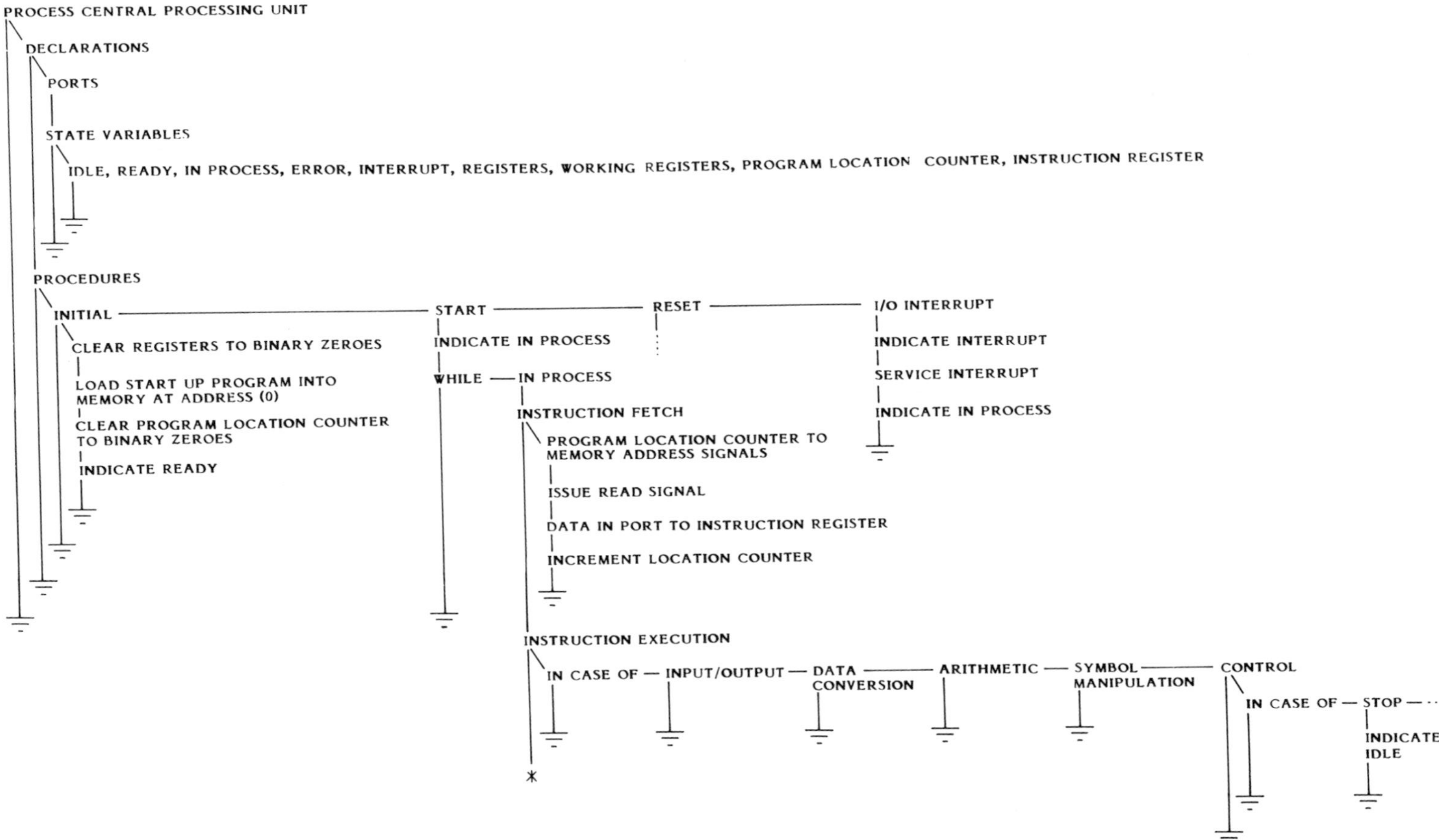
PROCESS CENTRAL PROCESSING UNIT
DECLARATIONS
PORTS
STATE VARIABLES
IDLE, READY, IN PROCESS, ERROR, INTERRUPT, REGISTERS, WORKING REGISTERS, PROGRAM LOCATION COUNTER, INSTRUCTION REGISTER
PROCEDURES
INITIAL
CLEAR REGISTERS TO BINARY ZEROES
LOAD START UP PROGRAM INTO MEMORY AT ADDRESS (0)
CLEAR PROGRAM LOCATION COUNTER TO BINARY ZEROES
INDICATE READY
START
INDICATE IN PROCESS
WHILE
IN PROCESS
INSTRUCTION FETCH
PROGRAM LOCATION COUNTER TO MEMORY ADDRESS SIGNALS
ISSUE READ SIGNAL
DATA IN PORT TO INSTRUCTION REGISTER
INCREMENT LOCATION COUNTER
INSTRUCTION EXECUTION
IN CASE OF
INPUT/OUTPUT
DATA CONVERSION
ARITHMETIC
SYMBOL MANIPULATION
CONTROL
IN CASE OF
STOP
INDICATE IDLE
RESET
I/O INTERRUPT
INDICATE INTERRUPT
SERVICE INTERRUPT
INDICATE IN PROCESS

CPU PROCESS LOGIC

Let us now consider the properties of each category of instruction; however, since it is not our purpose in this introductory book to build a complete picture of any particular computer system, we shall not describe all of the details of an instruction repertoire. We shall present a general description of the types of instructions in each category. Further, we shall illustrate the operation code and operand types without showing any detailed bit patterns or the ordering of operand fields.

Input/Output Instructions permit us to "read" data and programs from peripheral devices into the computer system memory and "write" data and programs from the memory to peripheral devices. The input/output controller as well as the CPU and memory processes become involved in the reading or writing.

Operation Code Field	Operand Fields
READ WRITE	Peripheral device address Memory address Count

The peripheral device address identifies which peripheral device is to be activated and used for the instruction execution. The memory address specifies the place in the memory where data is to be read into or written from. The count specifies the number of cells or bytes to be transmitted. **Note:** When new data or program instructions are read and placed into the memory, the previous contents of the memory cells are destroyed; however, when data or program instructions are written from the memory, the contents remain undisturbed and can be utilized in further processing.

Data read from terminals is always composed of a sequence of bytes; whereas, data read from storage type peripherals may already be in the form of internal binary signal representation. Most arithmetic facilities of CPU's are only equipped to perform arithmetic on binary values and not directly on bytes that may happen to have numeric values. To appreciate this difference, consider the representation of the number 13 as two bytes and as a binary number in the previous chapter.

Data Conversion Instructions permit us to convert arithmetic data (i.e. numbers) from their byte form (for example, in ASCII form) as a decimal number into internal binary format so that arithmetic operations can be performed upon the value. Conversely, to be able to display the results of computation, we must use a conversion instruction to convert from binary form to byte form prior to output transmission to a terminal screen or printing device.

Operation Code Field	Operand Fields
DECIMAL TO BINARY	Memory address source
BINARY TO DECIMAL	Memory address target
	Count

The memory address source gives the address of the value to be converted; whereas, the memory address target gives the address where the converted value is to be placed in the memory. The count field normally specifies the number of bytes of the source or target, respectively, for the two types of conversion instructions. **Note:** In most computer systems, a memory cell (word) consists of several bytes; for example, 2, 4, 6 or 8 bytes per cell are common quantities.

Register Loading and Storing Instructions permit us to fetch the contents of a particular memory cell (word) and place it into, "load," a register of the CPU and vice versa, that is, take the contents of a register and transmit it for "storing" into a particular memory cell. The loading is done in preparation for succeeding instructions to perform further processing (for example, to perform arithmetic operations). The storing is done to retain results of processing instructions.

Operation Code Field	Operand Fields
LOAD	Register address
STORE	Memory address

When loading a register, the memory address identifies the memory cell whose contents shall be loaded into the addressed register. **Note:** the previous contents of the register are "destroyed" upon loading; whereas, the content of the memory cell remains unchanged.

When storing from a register, the register address identifies the register whose contents shall be stored into the addressed memory cell. **Note:** the previous contents of the memory cell are "destroyed" upon storing; whereas, the contents of the register remain unchanged.

Arithmetic Instructions permit us to perform arithmetic on binary numbers which are contained in registers.

Operation Code Field	Operand Fields
CLEAR	Register address(es)
INCREMENT	
ADD	
SUBTRACT	
MULTIPLY	
DIVIDE	

The clear instruction allows us to place binary zeroes in every bit of the named register. The increment instruction is utilized to increment the named register by one (1). That is, one (1) is added to the current contents of the register. This counting type of capability is an important form of simple arithmetic. For addition, subtraction, multiplication and division, three register operands are involved. The first two operands name the registers that are to participate in the arithmetic operation and the third operand indicates where the resultant value is to be stored. **Note:** in many computer systems, only two operands are given and the result is stored in one of the two registers used as "inputs" to the arithmetic operation. Further, many computer systems permit one of the operands to be a memory cell instead of a register. However, for our purposes here, we shall assume that three registers are used for these four arithmetic operations.

Symbol Manipulation Instructions are provided to permit us to manipulate bytes (as, in ASCII format) in order to form "strings" of meaningful symbols.

Operation Code Field	Operand Fields
MOVE	Memory address source Memory address target Count

The move instruction allows us to join two strings of bytes together or to move bytes from within a string of bytes to another place in the memory. While other symbol manipulation instructions may exist in computer systems, the move instruction is the real work horse that allows us to edit and manipulate text inside the computer system, for example, in "word processing systems."

Control Instructions permit us to alter the sequence of instruction execution in the computer system. As described earlier, the CPU increments the PROGRAM LOCATION COUNTER by the length of the "current instruction" in order to determine the address of the "next instruction" to be fetched and executed. There are two types of control instructions: namely, **unconditional control instructions** which, when executed, cause a break in the sequence of instruction execution and **conditional control instructions** which can cause a break in the instruction sequence only if a conditional relationship between certain values exist. The unconditional instructions are as follows:

Operation Code Field	Operand Field
TRANSFER	Memory address
STOP	

The transfer instruction always specifies a memory address that is taken by the CPU and placed into the PROGRAM LOCATION COUNTER so that the next instruction to be executed is the instruction beginning at the named memory address and **not** the instruction following the transfer instruction. The execution of the stop instruction, as illustrated earlier, causes the CPU to reenter the IDLE state, thus breaking the instruction execution sequence.

Conditional control instructions are based upon the "testing" of a predicate relationship of two values (contents of registers and/or memory cells) and then only transferring control to a new place in the memory if the relationship exists (that is, if it is **true**).

Operation Code Field	Operand Field
EQUAL	Register address(es)
GREATER	Memory address(es)
LESS	

The meaning of equal, greater and less should be obvious. The first two operands name the register(s) and/or memory cell(s) whose contents are to be used as the operands for the comparison. A third operand is always a memory address which specifies the address to be placed into the PROGRAM LOCATION COUNTER in the case that the condition is "true". If the condition is "false", execution continues at the next instruction in sequence, namely, the instruction following the conditional control instruction.

Now that we have considered the general properties of an instruction repertoire, we can consider a collection of instructions that illustrate a program. The programming of a computer at this level is usually called **machine language programming** and we utilize a so-called "low level language" as mentioned in the previous chapter. The programs expressed in this low level language are called **assembly language** programs and they are translated by a translation system called the **assembler.** The "source program" (as described in the previous chapter) is represented as symbols which may be entered from a terminal. The following is not an assembly language program for any particular computer, but instead illustrates the use of the instructions we have considered in this chapter.

```
* DECLARATIONS
   PERIPHERAL DEVICES   TERMINAL KEYBOARD, TERMINAL SCREEN
   REGISTERS            SUM, COUNT, TEMPORARY
   MEMORY VARIABLES     IN VALUE, BINARY IN VALUE,
                        BINARY OUT VALUE, OUT VALUE

* PROCEDURE
*  INITIALIZATION
                 CLEAR (SUM)
                 CLEAR (COUNT)
*  PROCESSING
   REPEAT:       READ (TERMINAL KEYBOARD, IN VALUE, 2)
                 DECIMAL TO BINARY (IN VALUE, BINARY IN VALUE, 2)
                 LOAD (TEMPORARY, BINARY IN VALUE)
                 EQUAL (TEMPORARY, 99, FINAL)
                 ADD (SUM, TEMPORARY, SUM)
                 INCREMENT (COUNT)
                 TRANSFER (REPEAT)
   FINAL:        DIVIDE (SUM, COUNT, TEMPORARY)
                 STORE (TEMPORARY, BINARY OUT VALUE)
                 BINARY TO DECIMAL (BINARY OUT VALUE, OUT VALUE, 2)
                 WRITE (TERMINAL SCREEN, OUT VALUE, 2)
*  TERMINATE PROGRAM
                 STOP
```

The lines of the assembly language program that begin with an asterisk (*) are **comments** which help **us** to identify the structure of the program. In a manner similar to our higher level process description of the WASH process in chapter 5 and the CPU process in this chapter, we divide the assembly language program into "declaration" and "procedure" parts. The declarations, in this case, identify peripheral devices, registers and memory variables by names called **symbolic names** for the resources. When the assembler translates (assembles) the program, it will equate these names with real peripheral device addresses, register addresses and memory addresses. The bit patterns for these addresses are then utilized for placement into the instructions which use these objects in their operand fields.

The purpose of this illustrative program is to control the process of entering a sequence of numbers from the terminal keyboard which are to be summed up (added to each other) and then compute the average value by dividing the total sum by the number of values entered. When the program is assembled, it will exist purely as bit representations of operation codes and operands; namely an "object program" as mentioned in the previous chapter. The object program is then in "executable" format and may be interpreted by the CPU. When it is executed, the memory address of the first program instruction, namely that of the CLEAR (SUM) instruction, will be placed in the PROGRAM LOCATION

COUNTER. The reader should now examine this program by referring back to the descriptions of each type of instruction that appears in the program. The parentheses are used in the source program to identify the instruction operands. The symbolic names appearing prior to some of the instructions are called **labels** of the program. The reader should particularly observe the "processing" cycle in which a conditional control instruction is utilized to test if the current input value, taken from the terminal, is equal to the number 99. This number is called a **constant** and the assembler will assign a memory cell where the binary bit pattern for this constant will appear. The address of the constant is then placed in the operand field of the instruction. **Note:** we assume that all other numbers entered to be used in the calculation of an average are not equal to 99, which is utilized to identify the termination of the input sequence.

The concepts illustrated in the previous chapter and the current chapter provide a brief but comprehensive view of the essential aspects of the cooperating processes of a computer system. Your mastery of these two chapters will give you the proper background to further study the properties of computer system hardware and/or software or, as a layreader, to appreciate the central properties of computer system operation. You have undoubtedly observed that the properties of processes and systems with real life analogies, as presented in chapters 2 to 5, do not essentially change when we consider the cooperating processes of a computer system. It is mainly a question of the type and form of the objects (data) that are processed and the fact that we, via "programs," can convert the computer system into a "processor" of our application processes and systems. Once again, it is important to remember that the programs that we write are used to control the computer's operation. The computer is an obedient, extremely fast executor of our instructions. No more, no less.

Summary

In summary, the collection of cooperating processes in a computer system is referred to as the **configuration.** Some of the internal channels in the computer system are called **buses (highways).** The memory (store), as introduced in the previous chapter, provides a storage for data while they are not involved in processing and for the **instructions** of programs. The **Central Processing Unit** (CPU) is the main computational and symbol manipulating process of the computer system. The CPU is a stupid, but obedient "interpreter" of program instructions. The **Input/Output controller** maintains contact with the **peripheral devices,** which are the producers and consumers of data, including programs. The peripheral devices are connected to the I/O controller via **I/O channels.** Devices for storing large quantities of data and programs, devices to connect real physical processes to be controlled by the computer system, and terminals and printing devices are examples of peripheral devices.

The processors of the cooperating processes of a computer system are collectively referred to as the **computer hardware;** whereas, the programs contained in the computer's memory and in larger peripheral storage devices are called the **computer software.**

The **registers** of the CPU, the memory and the **I/O buffers** of the Input/Output controller are all local storages of their respective processes. These storage elements normally differ in size (capacity) and in their **access time.** Each register is identified via a **register address.** The memory is organized into **memory cells (words)** where each cell, similar to each register, is identified by a **memory address.** Memories of this type are referred to as **Random Access Memories** (RAM).

The signals, both data and control, are normally collected together and belong to the bus (highway) or I/O channel. Both serial and parallel transmission of data signals are used based upon the requirements for speed of transfer.

The connections between any two processes in a computer system is called the **interface** and the procedures followed in sending and receiving control signals and data across the interface is called the **protocol.** The signals of the interface are identified by **signal names.** In the connection between the CPU and the memory process, when "reading from" the memory, the **memory cell contents** are sent to the CPU but the contents remain unchanged in the memory as a result of the reading. Thus it is called a **non-destructive read.** When "writing to" the memory, the contents of the addressed memory cell are destroyed upon writing and is thus termed a **destructive write.** The connections between the CPU and Input/Output controller are utilized for the Input/Output protocol, where the CPU can request the reading of and the writing to peripheral devices as well as issue other **I/O control functions** to control the peripheral devices.

Each "instruction" recognized by the CPU contains an **operation code field** which identifies the type of instruction. The collection of instructions recognized by the CPU is called the **instruction repertoire.** Each instruction may contain one or more **operand fields** naming the objects to participate in the instruction execution. The details of the CPU which, as all processes, can be thought of as a "finite state machine," have been described along with the properties of the general categories of instructions: namely, **input/output instructions, data conversion instructions, arithmetic instructions, symbol** manipulation **instructions** and **control instructions.** The latter category is further subdivided into **unconditional control instructions** and **conditional control instructions.**

Programming of a computer system in terms of its basic instruction repertoire is called **machine language programming.** These programs are expressed in an **assembly language** and are translated via an **assembler.** An assembly language program can contain **comments** which help to identify important aspects of the program. The resources (peripheral devices, registers and memory variables) to be utilized by the program are given **symbolic names** by the programmer. Symbolic names are also utilized to identify **labels** of the program. The assembler assigns addresses of real resources to these symbolic names. **Constants** can be given as operand fields to which the assembler assigns memory addresses and creates the appropriate binary pattern for the constants.

Word List

Readers should verify their knowledge of this important chapter by reviewing the following terminology and referring back to the chapter text and/or summary as required.

configuration
instructions
Input/Output controller
I/O channels
computer software
I/O buffers
register address
memory address
interface
signal names
non-destructive read
I/O control functions
instruction repertoire
input/output instructions
register loading instructions
arithmetic instructions
control instructions
conditional instructions
assembly language
comments
labels
buses (highways)
central processing unit (CPU)
peripheral devices
computer hardware
registers
access time
memory cell (word)
Random Access Memories (RAM)
protocol
memory cell contents
destructive write
operation code field
operand fields
data conversion instructions
register storing instructions
symbol instructions
unconditional instructions
machine language programming
assembler
symbolic names
constants

Problems

1. Construct a process flowchart description of the memory process in the same form as the CPU process flowchart description. Use the memory read and memory write protocols given in this chapter in developing the process logic. Note: the logic must contain procedures for READ and WRITE.

2. Form a group of at least two and at most four people for the purpose of simulating the operation of the cooperating processes of a computer system. That is, the people will play the role of the computer hardware "processors." Use a large blackboard and draw pictures of the four cooperating processes presented in this chapter, including enough space for at least three registers in the CPU and a reasonably large number of memory cells. Assume that the assembly language program given in this chapter has been translated by an assembler and is to be executed beginning from memory address zero (0). This is the address of the first instruction. Each instruction of the program occupies one memory cell and memory cells for memory variables and constants appear following the last instruction cells. Follow through the successive changes of state of the processes when this program is executed and show the changes on your blackboard that result from the execution of each instruction.

3. Modify the assembly language program so that the value of the sum of all of the input values is written out to the terminal screen prior to writing the average value. Hint: you do not need to create any new memory variables since you can utilize BINARY OUT VALUE and OUT VALUE twice. Be careful about the order of their use.

4. Further modify the program so that each input value coming from the terminal keyboard is also displayed on the terminal screen, with the exception of the terminating value, namely, 99.

Chapter 8
MEMORIES AND PERIPHERAL DEVICES

In the previous chapter, we learned that a wide variety of peripheral devices can be attached to computer systems via "I/O channels." One of the purposes of this chapter is to present a categorization of the various types of peripheral devices and to illustrate some of their properties. However, first we shall consider some more details of how computer system memories are constructed.

During the history of computer systems, many different physical media have been utilized for realizing the memory process of the computer system. In this chapter we shall examine the two currently most utilized approaches to the memory hardware of the memory process. However, we should not forget that the "registers" of the CPU and the "I/O buffers" of the "Input/Output controller" are also memories that are local to these processes. Thus, we shall also consider the constitution of these "memory elements."

Magnetic Core Memories

In the mid-1950's, computer systems began to utilize a form of memory technology called **magnetic core memory.** This form has been successively improved since its introduction and still exists as an important memory technology in modern day computer systems. It has some unique properties which give it advantages over other approaches. The purpose of a magnetic core memory, as with all memory devices, is to be able to retain the state representing binary 0 or binary 1 in a more permanent fashion than we have illustrated previously when we have discussed the transmission and processing of binary signals. In a magnetic core memory, the term "magnet" is an important aspect since we utilize small circular metallic elements, **cores,** which are magnets that can be polarized to positive or negative conditions, thus giving us the possibility to represent the two states of binary 0 and binary 1. The magnetic core elements are extremely small and are placed in an "array" structure as illustrated in the following picture.

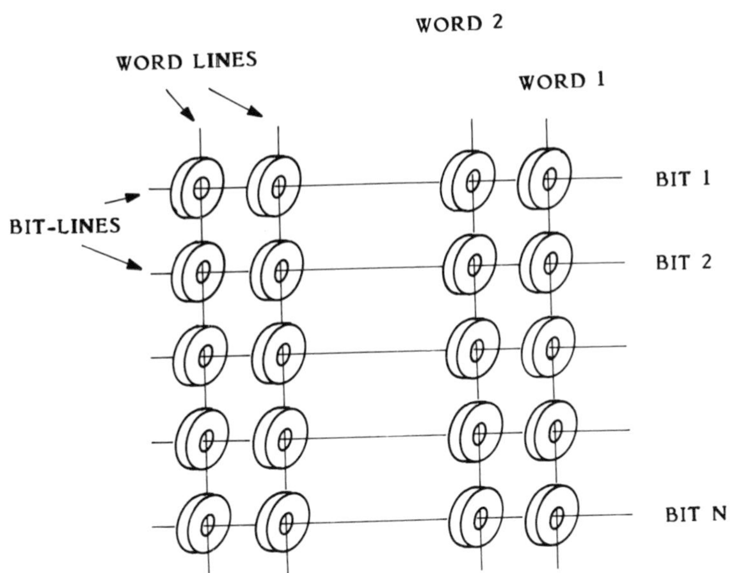

MAGNETIC CORE MEMORY

Each of the circular elements in this picture is a magnetic core, as mentioned above. Three small wires pass through each core in the memory; however, in this picture we represent two of the wires. One of these lines is used to identify the word position to be read from or written into and the other line, the selection of particular bit positions within the word. The third wire is a sense wire that goes through all cores and is used for reading out and changing core states. By activating a particular word line and all bit lines, along with the use of the sense line, one is able to operate upon a complete memory word. The logic of the memory process activates these operations in order to provide the memory process activities of reading and writing. It is important to note with magnetic core memory, since the elements are indeed magnets, that even if the electric power for the computer system is turned off, the state of the memory is retained in that the magnetic cores retain their positive or negative condition at the time of the loss of power. This is an important property in many systems and is not available in the second type of commonly utilized memory that we are about to discuss.

Semiconductor Memories

An important technology utilized in realizing the memories of computer systems, including registers and I/O buffers, is **semiconductor memories.** These memories are composed of so-called **flip/flop** elements (synonymously called **latches)** which are illustrated as a process in the following picture.

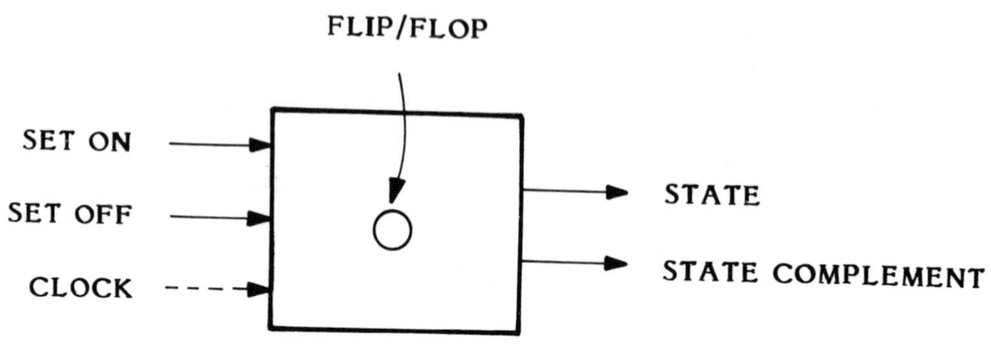

A FLIP/FLOP ELEMENT

The circle in the center of the flip/flop process is utilized to illustrate the flip/flop which is, in reality, realized with "transistors" of semiconductor materials. The details of how such flip/flops are constructed will be presented in the following chapter. However, suffice it to say that this simple element can retain one of two values, either "on" or "off," representing the binary value 1 or the binary value 0. To simplify our understanding of this element, we can imagine that the circle is a light that when turned on represents a binary 1 and when turned off represents a binary 0. We utilize two input signals, one to set the flip/flop on and another to set the flip/flop off. The time at which the flip/flop is set is determined by the receiving of a clock signal in the same manner as we discussed when we explained the structure of a "synchronous control" mechanism, in chapter 4. At the time of the clock signal, the flip/flop is set, and shortly thereafter the value of the flip/flop is available at the output ports for use outside of the flip/flop memory. This "current" state is available in two forms: namely, the true current state of the flip/flop and the so-called **complement** of the flip/flop state. The complement simply means the "opposite" value; for example, if the state of the flip/flop is set to one (1) then the complement is zero (0); otherwise if the flip/flop is set to zero (0) then the complement is one (1). This detail is unimportant at this point in time but is an important property for the hardware logic of computer systems to be discussed in the following chapter.

To be completely precise about the operation of a flip/flop element, let us consider the following dimensional flowchart which illustrates the structure of the flip/flop process logic.

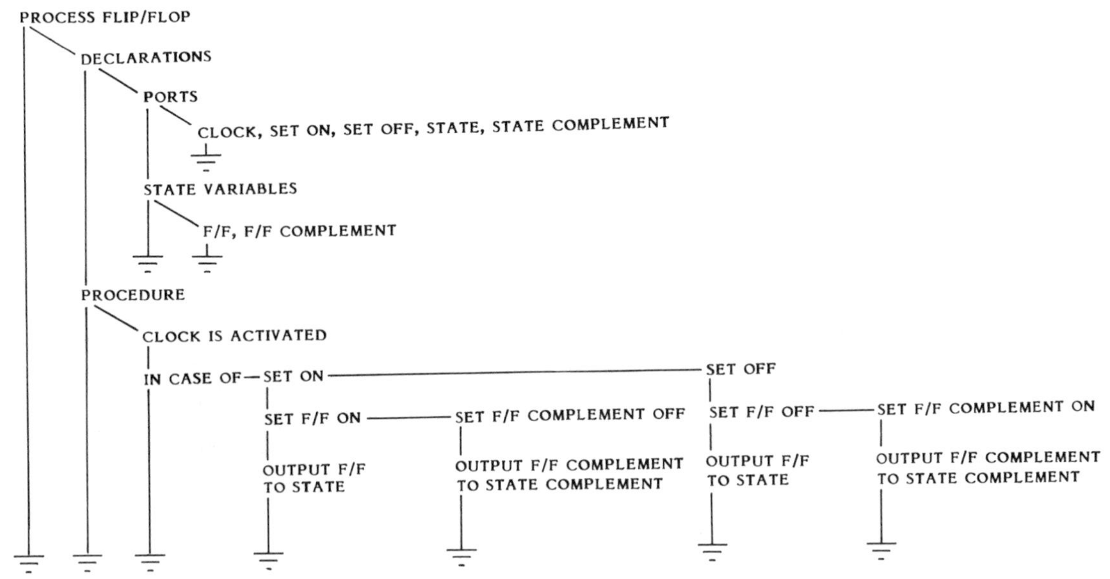

A FLIP/FLOP PROCESS DESCRIPTION

Here we enumerate the input and output ports as well as the flip/flop element and its complement as state variables. The only procedure of the process is that of a clock signal occurrance. When the clock signal is present, we see that we do two different things based upon whether the SET ON signal is given or the SET OFF signal is given. An important new idea in this dimensional flowchart is the introduction of **parallel sequences;** namely, when we request to SET ON the flip/flop, both the setting on and the complement setting of the flip/flop are performed simultaneously, that is, in parallel. Further the two states are also available in parallel. Parallel execution of process logic of this type is an important property in computer "hardware" where in order to improve the speed of logic execution, we attempt to accomplish as many activities in parallel as possible. The introduction of parallel sequences is an extension of the dimensional flowcharting conventions introduced in chapter 5. To be complete, we introduce the general structure of parallel sequences in the following picture.

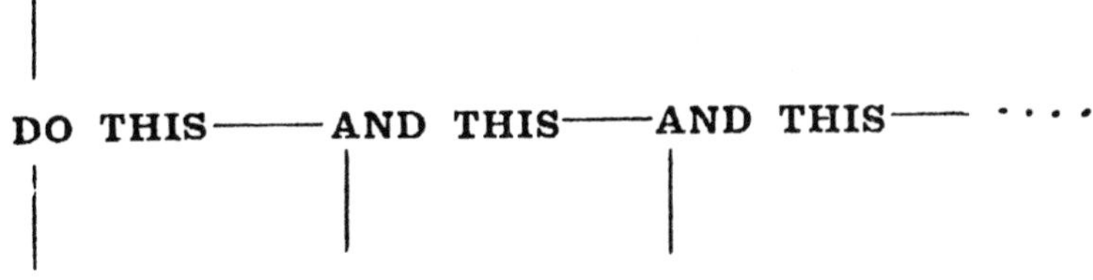

PARALLEL SEQUENCES

Flip/flop elements are collected together to form an "array" of flip/flops in order to constitute registers in the CPU, I/O buffers in the Input/Output controller or in the case of the memory process, the memory cells (words). To illustrate this property, let us consider the following picture of a four bit flip/flop memory.

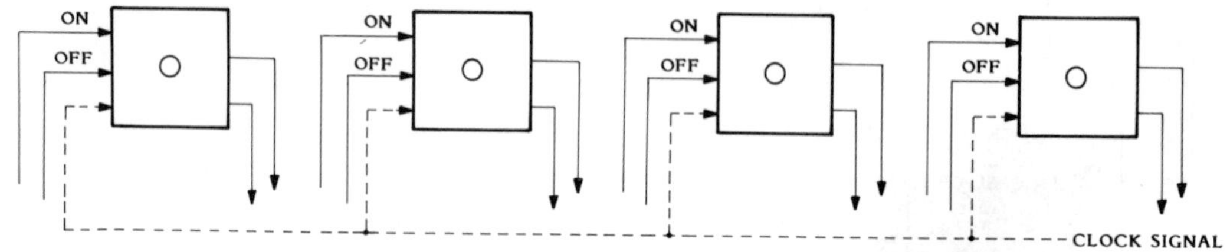

AN ARRAY OF FLIP/FLOPS

Here we can observe that the clock signal, mentioned earlier, is delivered to all flip/flop process elements simultaneously. Consequently each of the positions of the array are set based upon current value of their SET ON or SET OFF input lines. Thus, every time the clock signal is set on, the array elements will be set to a new current state. Shortly thereafter, the current new state of each element of the array and its complement are available for other process logic. For example, in the case of registers in the CPU, they may be used as inputs for arithmetic computations.

The use of flip/flops as a basic element of the semiconductor memories of computer system memory processes became extremely important during the 1970's, particularly with the introduction of the so-called "Large Scale Integration" (LSI). In LSI many flip/flops can be realized with transistors in an extremely small physical space and at extremely low costs per bit. Thousands of bits can be constructed on a surface no larger than about one-fourth the size of a common postage stamp. These memories have enabled major advances in storage technology such that quantities of memories up into the millions of bits are now easily attainable. However, one should realize that an important difference between the use of semiconductor memories and magnetic core memories is that with semiconductor memories, when power is taken away from the computer system, the state of the flip/flops is destroyed. This means that we are not able to restart the computer system when power is available again with the state of the memory intact. As mentioned earlier, since magnets are used in the magnetic core memory, they retain their state when power is taken away from the computer system and restarting the system is possible with the previous state of the memory intact. Thus, when using semiconductor memories, care must be taken in the total computer system design to see to it that critical data and/or program instructions are not lost as a result of power failure.

Storage Peripherals

As mentioned in the previous chapters, the memory of the memory process is of limited capacity even if we consider memories of several million bits. Consequently, we normally cannot store all data and programs in the memory process at the same time. Instead, we utilize peripheral storage devices to retain the large bulk quantities of data and programs. In this section we shall consider two such media for retaining large quantities of information, namely **magnetic tapes** and **magnetic discs.** In both of these media, the data or programs are structured on the media in the form of so-called **files.** The files are further sub-divided into units of data and/or programs called **records.** We can use the analogy of a "file" being a folder that we keep in a filing cabinet and a "record" as being each paper within the folder. Records recorded on a magnetic tape or disc file could well be the same organization as a "structure" described in the discussion of data structures in chapter 6; however in this context, records normally refer to sequences of data or program instructions as they are physically organized on the external storage media. A record may contain related or unrelated scalar values, an entire array or part of an array, a structure or several structures, all or part of the instructions of a program or even a mixture of these elements.

Let us now consider the properties of magnetic tape peripheral devices. The recording of data and/or programs in the form of bit-patterns on the magnetic tape surface, the **tape reel** and the device used to write and read a tape, namely the **tape drive** are illustrated in the following picture.

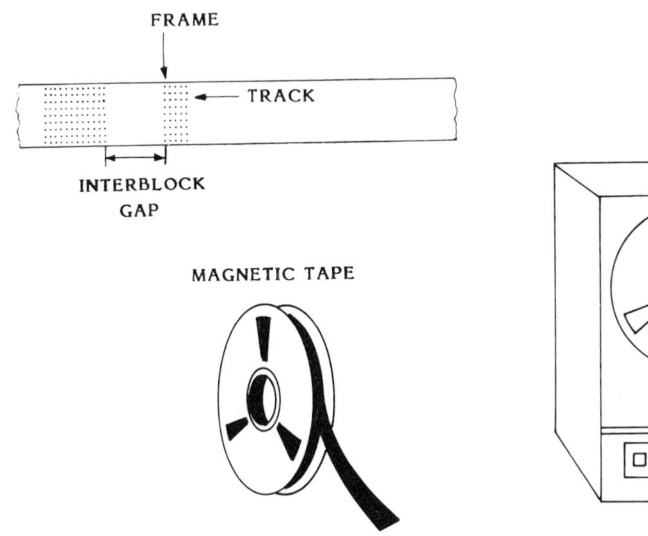

TAPE REEL

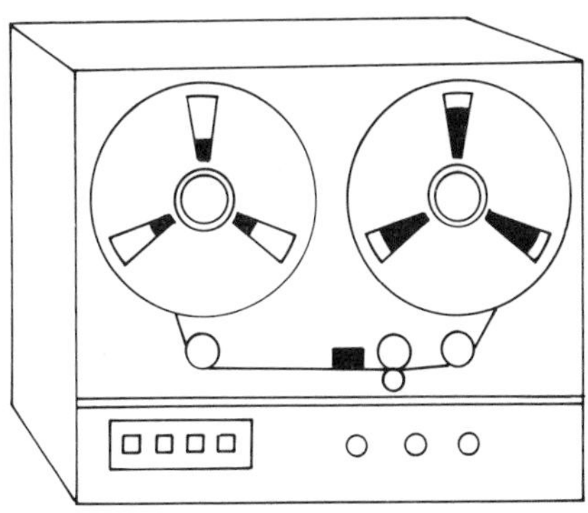

TAPE DRIVE

Again we should observe the use of the word magnet. The material used for magnetic tapes is such that individual spots on the tape can be altered between two states (conditions) representing, once again, the binary values one (1) and zero (0). Each dot that we see on the magnetic tape strip can represent one of these two values. Records on the magnetic tape are normally grouped into **blocks** of one or more records and the blocks are separated by **inter-block gaps,** that is, places where no recording takes place. The termination of a file on the magnetic tape is indicated by an **end of file** mark which is a special bit pattern recorded onto the tape. Data stored on magnetic tapes can be represented by the form of symbols from a character set (as, ASCII symbols) or represented as binary data values.

In examining the tape strip that was illustrated, you will notice that the bits are organized in groups of 9 elements. Thus, this tape is called a 9 channel tape. When recording is in the form of ASCII symbols, each symbol occupies 8 of the bits thus forming a "byte" as described earlier. The ninth bit is used for error control purposes and is called the **parity bit.** The amount of data and/or programs stored on a magnetic tape is based upon the so-called **recording density;** that is the number of bytes that can be placed in an "inch" of magnetic tape and, of course, the length of the tape. Consequently we normally refer to recording at the rate of, for example, 800 bpi or 1600 bpi, where bpi means **bytes per inch.** The device used for writing and reading magnetic tape, namely, the tape drive as illustrated above, contains a **read/write head** which is used for the actual physical process of recording information onto the magnetic tape or for reading from the magnetic tape. We can view this peripheral device as a process and therefore as a finite state machine with push buttons used to manually activate related physical processes and lights to illustrate the device state. When actively connected to the computer system, the tape drive is controlled by commands given from the program via the CPU and Input/Output controller, which tells it when to read and when to write and can provide other commands telling it, for example, to rewind the tape or to space the tape forwards or backwards a certain number of blocks.

The recording of the records within blocks on a magnetic tape occurs one after another, in sequence; consequently, we call the files retained on magnetic tape media **sequential files.** In processing sequential files we normally process the file in the order in which the records appear on the magnetic tape media.

Another very important file structure is the so-called **random access file.** In this case we do not have to store the records of the file in a sequential order. Such files are organized so that a **record key** is utilized to identify (i.e. address) each individual record in the file. The device then "seeks" to find this record. Further, when the program wishes to process an individual record from this file, the desired key (contained in one or more memory cells) is sent via the CPU and Input/Output controller to the peripheral device. Further commands are given to read and/or write this particular record within the file. This random access file property is available when we utilize "**magnetic discs.**" Magnetic discs appear very much like phonograph records and, similar to phonographs, an arm is utilized; however, in the case of magnetic discs it is used to both read and write from the disc surfaces. The basic structure of discs, their physical organization and the device used for controlling disc operations are illustrated in the following picture.

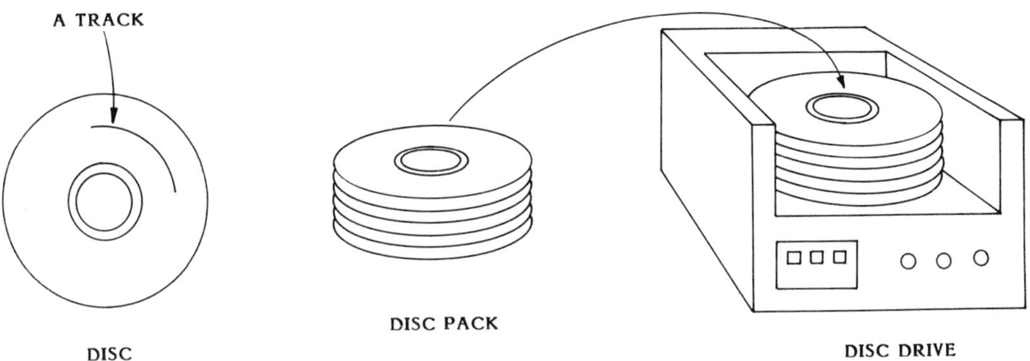

The disc surface is organized into so-called **tracks** where data and/or program records are magnetically recorded. A number of discs are collected together to form a **disc pack.** This disc pack is then mounted into a **disc drive.** The disc drive contains arms with read/write heads that are utilized to record "write" information on the tracks of selected disc surfaces and read information from disc surfaces. Further, the arm is used to search for the keys related to the individual records of the random access file. A disc pack, of this variety, normally contains several hundred or even a few thousand files. Disc drives can be utilized to store extremely large quantities of information; hundreds of millions of bytes of information can be retained on some of the larger types of disc packs.

Another less expensive disc technology and a very practical one in many environments, particularly for low cost computer systems, is the use of a so-called **floppy disc.** The floppy disc is not hard as the other discs but is thin and flexible and is the same size as a 45 rpm record. Consequently, they are easily transportable and they can be placed into the so-called **floppy disc drive.** Addressing properties as well as recording techniques are similar to those of the larger disc drives. However, we cannot retain as much information on floppy discs; we can store hundreds of thousands of bytes of information instead of being able to store millions of bytes of information. A floppy disc and its disc drive are illustrated as follows:

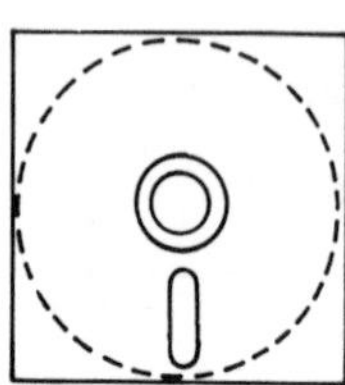

FLOPPY DISC

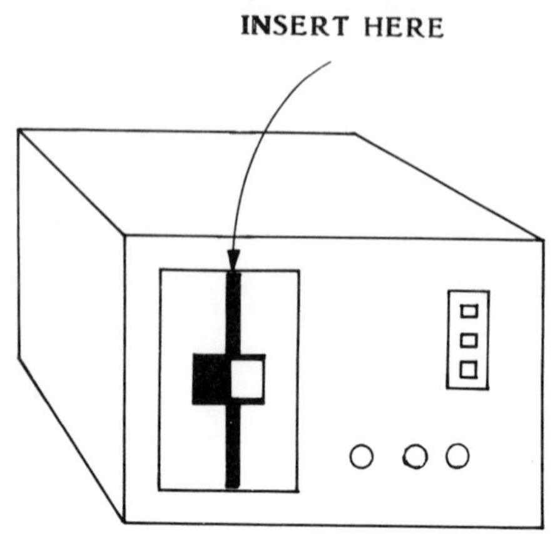

FLOPPY DISC DRIVE

The presentation of storage peripherals given here is simply a sampling of the variety of devices available. Amongst many other devices in this category, we can name **cassette tapes** and **cassette tape drives,** similar to those we use for recorded music, which can be used for small sequential files; and **magnetic drums** in which a rotating cylinder with related read/write head logic is used in larger computer systems to store large numbers of randomly accessible files with very rapid "access." Within the magnetic disc category, there exist the **moving head drives** as described earlier, in which a moving **disc arm** containing a read/write head is used for each disc surface, and **fixed head drives** which use one disc arm per track. This latter form of disc drive provides for very rapid access to keyed records since searching is performed within a single track and not over all of the tracks of a surface.

Peripherals to Control Physical Processes

An important property of computer systems is the ability to control physical processes from a program residing in the computer system. This can involve, for example, controlling motors, controlling the movement of goods in a production line, controlling chemical processes, controlling power production and distribution, etc. To illustrate some basic features of this type of control, let us consider the following picture that illustrates a basin filled with water in which a thermometer is used to measure the water temperature and a heating element to heat up the water.

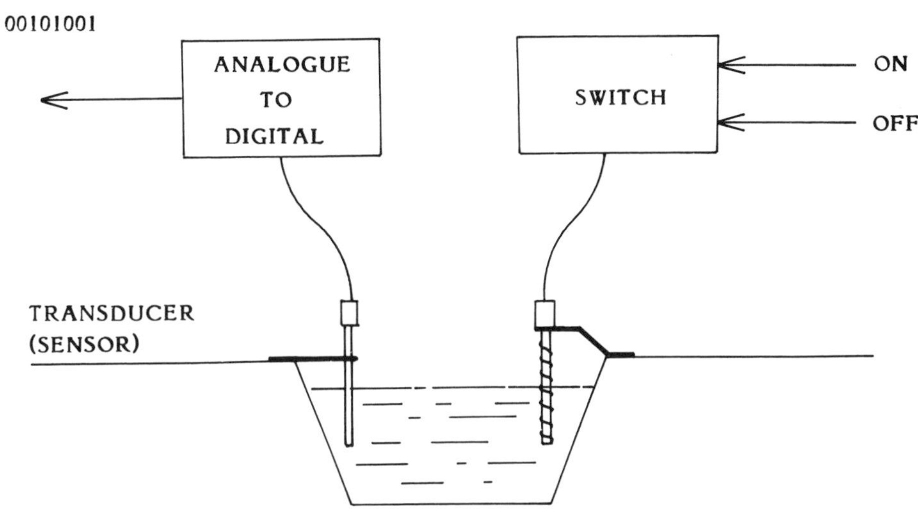

PERIPHERALS FOR CONTROLLING A PHYSICAL PROCESS

We could perhaps view this basin as the basin used in our dish processing system. The thermometer is part of a so-called **transducer** and a synonymous word is **sensor.** It is possible for us to read the temperature level of the thermometer as a so-called **analogue signal.** An analogue signal is constituted as a voltage level that is proportional to a measured quantity, in this case temperature. Digital computer systems are not equipped to directly process analogue signals. Thus the analogue signal, which indicates the temperature level, must be converted into digital signals to be sent further to the computer system by an **analogue to digital converter.** In the picture, we see the conversion resulting in a string of bits representing the temperature value. This value is "inputted" into the computer system where the program, for example, tests to see if the temperature is sufficiently high. The computer program can, based upon this decision, selectively turn on or turn off the heating element by "outputting" a signal to a switch which then controls this element. In this case, we utilize a very simple control device for switching to the on or off condition. There are devices which convert a digital output signal to an analogue signal which are called **digital to analogue converters** and which can be used for controlling, for example, the speed of a motor. A wide variety of physical processes are controlled by computer systems in today's world. This type of application of computer systems is called **process control.** In its advanced forms, it is the basis for so-called "industrial robots" that hopefully will take over the monotonous and dangerous jobs from humans. The hope is that this trend will not reduce employment opportunities but provide for new industrial employment categories.

Printing Peripheral Devices

It is obviously important that we receive outputs from computer systems in a form which we humans can interpret; therefore, an important type of peripheral device is the **printer.** The quality of printed text of various printing devices varies quite widely based upon the technology utilized. In the following picture we illustrate two printing devices, namely, a so-called **high speed printer** and a more conventional looking typewriter, or **printing terminal** that is connected to the computer system as a peripheral device.

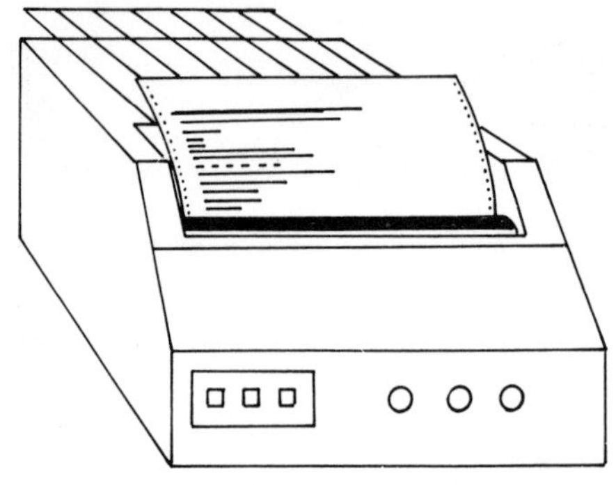

HIGH SPEED PRINTER

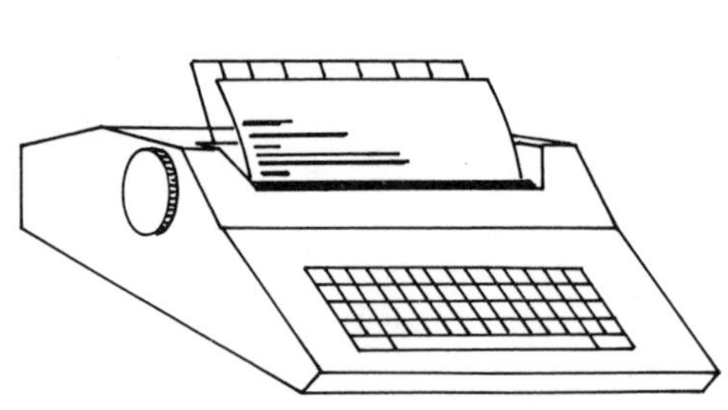

PRINTING TERMINAL

The high speed printer is normally utilized for printing large quantities of information where the quality of the print style is not the important aspect. If we wish to produce a high quality document, we can utilize the printing terminal connected to the computer system in order to produce text of equal quality to that produced by a conventional typewriter. In fact, this book was printed on this type of device.

The area of computer printer technology is one in which many new imaginative inventions have already taken place and more will undoubtedly be forthcoming. In reality, high speed printers are available that can also produce as good quality print as conventional typewriters and in many cases, even better. However, these devices are quite expensive. Some printing devices provide for photo-composition in which case many different type "fonts" can be utilized and, in fact, intermixed in the same document (for example, the use of italic characters to differentiate or stress important words).

Other Peripheral Devices

The variety of peripheral devices that have been connected to computer systems or could be connected is too voluminous to begin to enumerate in this introductory book. We have covered in this chapter some of the major types and in previous chapters have already considered the all important "computer terminal" with its keyboard and screen. The terminal is the peripheral device via which the majority of computer users have their "human/machine communication." A wide variety of terminals exist and the technology is moving rapidly forward in this area.

In order to complement our list of peripheral devices with at least a few more important peripherals we should mention **graphic terminals** which can be utilized to draw pictures and/or diagrams under the control of a program. Diagrams and pictures are also available in "hard copy" form via **digital plotters** which can include large engineering drawings. Such devices are also utilized to produce "computer art."

Summary

In this chapter, we have considered the general properties of some memories and some peripheral devices. **Magnetic core memories** are composed of arrays of small circular magnets called **cores** which can be magnetized and thus are capable of representing the two states binary 1 and binary 0. Addressing wires for selecting words and bit positions as well as a sense line wire for reading and writing are placed through the "cores." Magnetic core memories retain their state even if power is taken away from the computer system. Another important memory type which is realized via "transistors" are **semiconductor memories** composed of **flip/flops (latches)** where each **flip/flop** can be utilized to represent the two states binary 1 and binary 0 as long as power is supplied to the computer system. In addition to retaining the true state of the flip/flop, the **complement** (opposite state) is retained and made available as a flip/flop output. In computer hardware processes, the logic is frequently organized so that **parallel sequences** of logic can be executed at the same time. The representation of parallel sequences as a dimensional flowchart convention has been illustrated. In the past, flip/flops have largely been used for memories of small sizes (e.g., registers and buffers); however, with the introduction of "Large Scale Integration" (LSI) in the 1970's, large quantities of flip/flops (realized as transistors via semiconductor materials) could be produced economically.

The two major types of storage peripherals are **magnetic tapes** and **magnetic discs.** Data or programs recorded on these media are organized into **files** and the files are further subdivided into **records.** In the case of magnetic tape, the tape is contained on a **tape reel,** and a **tape drive** is used for writing onto or reading from the tape. Records on magnetic tape are normally grouped into **blocks** of records and the blocks are separated by **inter-block gaps.** The termination of the file is indicated by an **end of file** mark. The recording of bytes (8 bits) on a tape requires the use of a ninth **parity bit** which is used for error control purposes. Further, the amount of data or program instructions (in terms of bytes) that can be recorded on the tape depends upon the **recording density** which is expressed in bpi, namely, **bytes per inch.** The mechanism of the tape drive that reads and writes from/onto tapes is called the **read/write head.** Files retained on magnetic tapes are called **sequential files** since the records are stored one after another and are normally processed in the order in which they appear in the file. Another type of file called a **random access file** permits the use of **record keys** to identify (i.e. address) individual records and therefore permits random access to individual records of files much like Random Access Memories (RAM) permit random access to memory cells (words) based upon their address as a key. This type of file is available when utilizing "magnetic discs." The disc surface is organized into **tracks** and a number of disc surfaces form a **disc pack** which can be mounted into a **disc drive.** The disc drive contains arms which have read/write heads used for searching, reading and writing on the disc surfaces. **Floppy discs** are a low cost disc technology in which a single flexible disc is placed into a **floppy disc drive** which has an arm for the searching, reading and writing operations. Other forms of storage peripherals mentioned include **cassette tapes** and **cassette tape drives** as well as **magnetic drums.** Within the magnetic disc technology, there exist **moving head drives** (as presented in this chapter) and **fixed head drives** which have a higher performance.

Peripheral devices are available which assist in controlling physical processes via the computer system. We need to have measuring instruments, namely **transducers (sensors)**, that measure process related features, for example, temperature, pressure, etc. This measurement is in the form of an **analogue signal** which is converted to binary signals via an **analogue to digital converter** prior to entry to the computer system. Likewise, binary signals can be sent to a **digital to analogue converter** where the resultant analogue signal controls, for example, motor speed. This type of computer system application is called **process control.**

In providing outputs that we humans can examine, we can utilize a **printer** as a peripheral device. A **high speed printer** may produce printed output quickly but be of inferior quality; whereas, a **printing teminal** can produce quality equal to conventional typewriters. Some more expensive photo-composition printers can produce high quality at high speeds but, of course, also at greater cost.

The terminal, composed of the terminal keyboard and the terminal screen, is probably the most widespread peripheral. A **graphic terminal** which permits the composition of pictures and **digital plotters** which can create drawings are two other important peripheral devices aimed at improving the human/machine communication.

Word List

Readers should review the following word list in order to solidify their understanding of the basic memory and peripheral device concepts and terminology presented in this chapter.

magnetic core memories	cores
semiconductor memories	flip/flop (latch)
complement	parallel sequences
magnetic tapes	magnetic discs
files	records
tape reel	tape drive
blocks	inter-block gap
end of file	parity bit
recording density	bytes per inch (bpi)
read/write head	sequential files
random access files	record keys
tracks	disc pack
disc drive	floppy disc
floppy disc drive	cassette tape
cassette tape drive	magnetic drums
moving head drive	fixed head drive
transducers (sensors)	analogue signal
analogue to digital converter	digital to analogue converter
process control	printer
high speed printer	printing terminal
graphic terminal	digital plotter

Problems

1. Assume that a positive condition (+) is used to represent a binary 1 and a negative condition (-) is used to represent a binary 0 in each core of the magnetic core memory. Indicate, beside each core of WORD 1 and WORD 2 of the core memory picture given in this chapter, the equivalent of the binary values 10110 and 01010 for WORD 1 and WORD 2, respectively. What are the equivalent decimal values for these five bit binary values?

2. Imagine that the circles indicated in the flip/flop memory array picture are lights and that a binary 1 is indicated by the light being "on", whereas a binary 0 is represented by the light being "off". Using this picture, fill in the sequence of on and off lights in the picture to correspond to the pattern 1101. What is the equivalent decimal value for this binary value?

3. Again utilizing the picture of the four bit flip/flop memory array, circle the SET ON and SET OFF lines that must be active at the time of a clock signal in order to change the state of flip/flop memory array to the binary value 0110. When this value is placed in the state of the memory, what are the complement values of each flip/flop?

4. In chapter 6, the 7 bit ASCII encodings for the following message were given. Assuming that the two bits prior to each encoding are both binary zeroes, draw a picture of a 9 channel magnetic tape strip and indicate the recorded bit patterns for this message.

Value is 13.

Circle the bits that are to be binary 1 (magnetized).

5. Create a picture of a process called MONITOR which monitors the water temperature in the process control example given in this chapter. The binary signal from the analogue to digital converter is received at its input port as well as a clock signal which tells the process when to monitor the temperature. Ignore initial and reset signals. Two output ports are used for connection to the switch which turns the heating element on and off. Assume that we want to keep the temperature above 55 degrees Centigrade. Create a process description in the form of a dimensional flowchart of this MONITOR process which includes the required declarations and procedures. Note: only one procedure is required, namely, the procedure required for the CLOCK signal occurrance.

Chapter 9
DIGITAL PROCESSES

In this chapter, we shall consider the basic elements utilized in constructing the hardware "processors" that execute the cooperating processes of the computer system. We shall observe that the most basic of these "digital processes" are indeed almost trivial and it is the combination of many such processes that makes the computer system seemingly complex.

ONE PERSON'S PROCESSES ARE ANOTHER PERSON'S PROCESSOR

The author

We implied in the introductory paragraph that digital processes are utilized to create the hardware processors. From the point of view of those who design and construct computers, they work with building cooperating digital processes which, when constructed, are viewed by the "user" of these cooperating processes as a processor of their "application" processes. Consequently the collection of cooperating digital processes becomes the processors for the memory Central Processing Unit, Input/Output Controller and the peripheral device processes.

Basic Gating Processes

Digital processes are designed to process signals of the binary type as described in chapter 6. The following three processes lie at the heart of all digital signal processing in computer systems.

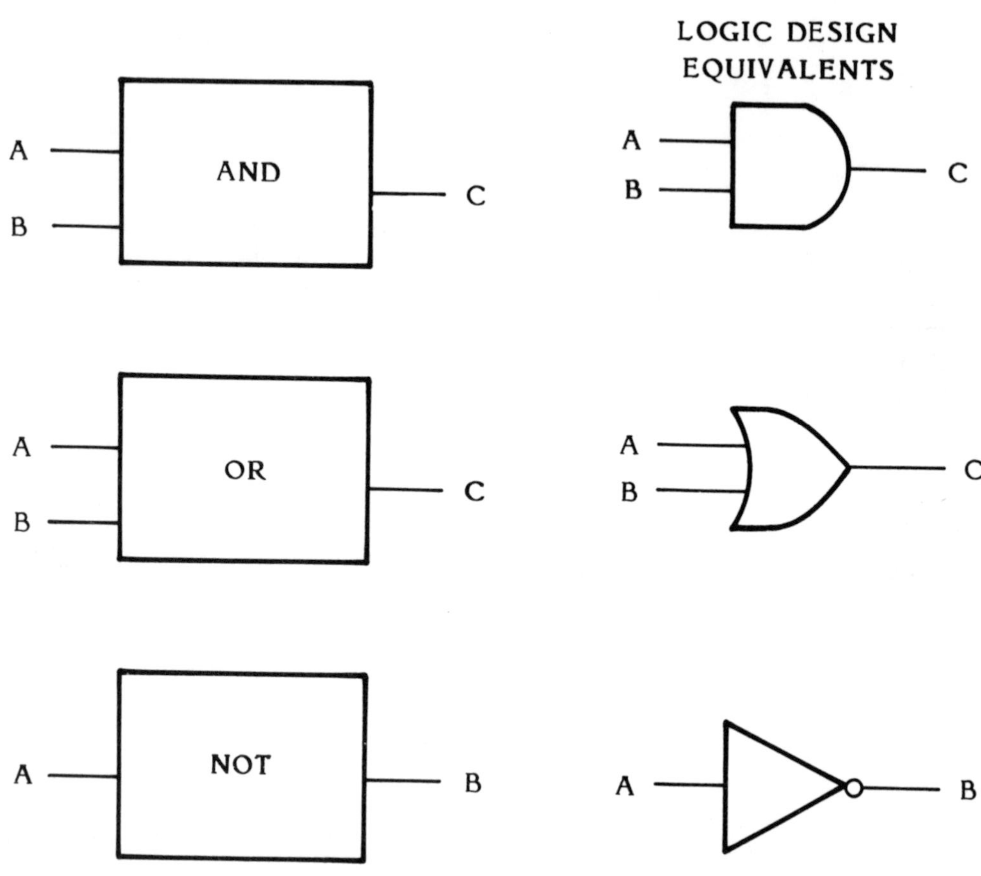

BASIC DIGITAL PROCESSES

The process pictures at the left are familiar to us as processes having ports for process inputs and outputs used for receiving and sending digital signals. Each process input can contain a binary 0 (voltage level 0) or a binary 1 (voltage level +2), assuming the representation presented in chapter 6. Likewise, the process output is a resulting binary signal. We call such digital processes **gates** which are the building blocks of **logic design.** Logic designers (the builders of cooperating digital processes) normally utilize the notation given to the right as their representation of these basic processes, but this in no way alters our view of them as processes. The three gates illustrated here are called the **AND gate,** the **OR gate** and the **NOT gate,** respectively.

The process logic of these three processes (gates) is utterly simple and is given as follows.

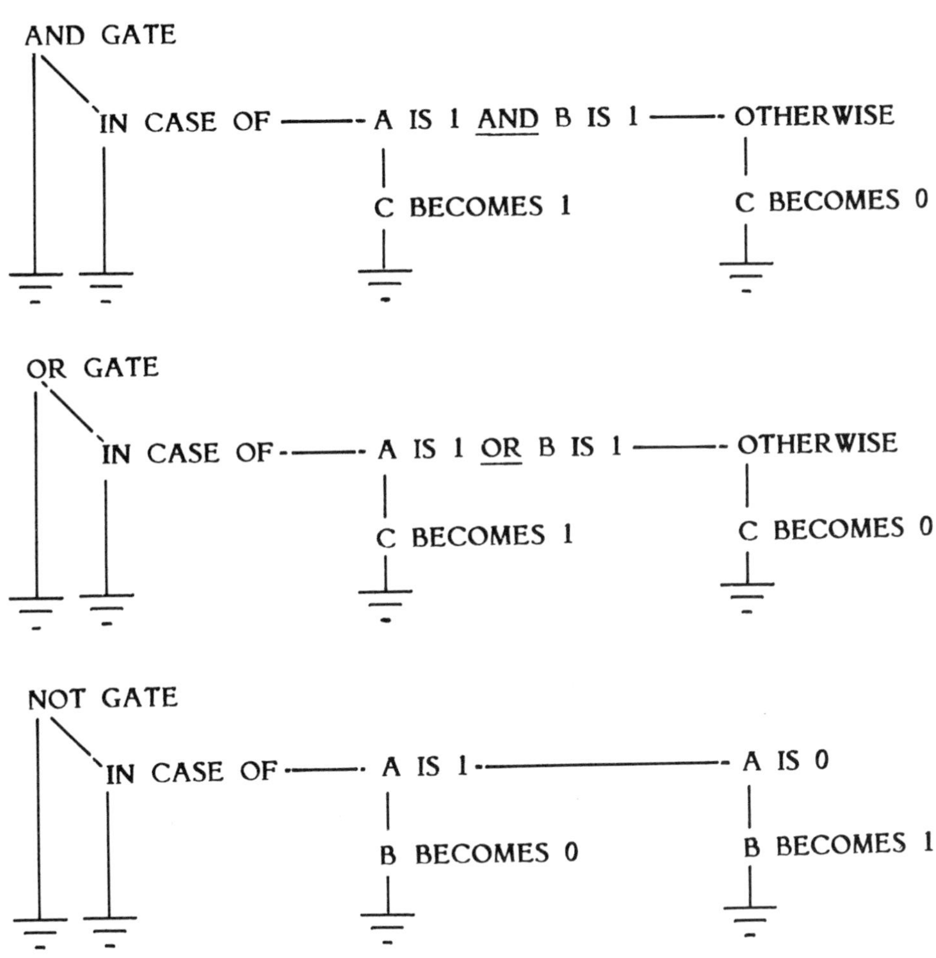

PROCESS LOGIC FOR GATES

Boolean Algebra and Computer Arithmetic

A very important property of these basic digital processes is that the possible inputs and outputs are "very finite," namely binary 0 or binary 1. Consequently, if we examine the logic of the processes carefully, we may make a complete enumeration of all possible inputs and outputs as follows.

SIGNAL VALUES

GATE	A	B	C
AND	0	0	0
	0	1	0
	1	0	0
	1	1	1
OR	0	0	0
	0	1	1
	1	0	1
	1	1	1
NOT	0	1	
	1	0	

ENUMERATION OF ALL POSSIBLE
GATE INPUTS AND OUTPUTS

For the AND and OR gates, remember A and B are the inputs and C is the output; whereas, for the NOT gate A is the single input and B the output. One may ask the question: what do these trivial processes have to do with this seemingly complex capability of computers to perform arithmetic at amazing speeds? The answer is that arithmetic on binary numbers can be performed according to the very simple operations of the **Boolean algebra**(*) in which only these three operations (and, or and not) are permitted. Further, we can prove that these operations are sufficient as we shall shortly demonstrate. Let us first consider the addition of two decimal digits followed by the addition of two binary digits to show that the arithmetic principles of these two number bases are the same.

(*) George Boole was an English mathematician who presented the algebra that bears his name in 1854.

Some examples of decimal addition are as follows.

```
 A      0     0     6     7     8
+B     +0    +5    +0    +2    +5
---    ---   ---   ---   ---   ---
 C      0     5     6     9    13
                               ^
                               |__ CARRY
```

EXAMPLES OF RESULTS OF ADDING TWO DECIMAL DIGITS

We label the inputs to the addition A and B and the result of the addition C. Observe that in the last example, that in addition to producing a decimal digit for C, a "carry" of 1 is produced. We know that a carry is to be produced due to the fact that the result exceeds the highest possible value in the alphabet of decimal numbers; namely 9. Let us now consider the addition of two binary digits as follows.

```
 A      0     0     1     1
+B     +0    +1    +0    +1
---    ---   ---   ---   ---
 C      0     1     1    10
                         ^
                         |__ CARRY
```

ALL POSSIBLE RESULTS OF ADDING TWO BINARY DIGITS

In this case, the highest possible value in the alphabet of binary numbers is 1. Consequently, when the result of adding two binary digits exceeds 1, as in the decimal case for 9, a carry of 1 is produced in addition to the resulting binary digit C. While we have only illustrated some examples of decimal arithmetic, we have enumerated "all" possible results of adding two binary digits A and B.

The reader may now ask the question: How can binary values of greater than one digit of precision be added together? The principle of using "carries" from each digit to the next digit position follows exactly the same principles as in decimal arithmetic. To illustrate this point, let us consider two binary additions, one which does not produce any carries and a second which produces carries as follows.

A	1000	equivalent to	8	0111	equivalent to	7
+B	+0101	"	+5	+0110	"	+6
C	1101	"	13	1101	"	13

ADDITION OF SEVERAL BINARY DIGITS

In the first addition, no carries are produced so the result of each C output digit is the result of each digit addition. In the second example, two carries are produced as indicated by the arrows. Notice that when we add (1+1+1 as carry) we get 1 as the C result for that digit plus a new carry to the next position. Compare this with some of your own examples of decimal addition that generate carries and create some of your own binary addition examples.

We have observed that arithmetic on positive binary integer values is possible. Computer systems also are equipped to perform arithmetic on negative values and on fractional values but we shall not consider these mechanisms in this introductory book.

It is important to note that the finite nature of binary arithmetic resulting in limited combinations of binary 0's and 1's is the basis for the use of the and, or and not logic of Boolean algebra for performing binary arithmetic. We shall illustrate these principles in the following section.

Digital Circuits

Through the use of combinations of cooperating digital processes (gates), we can construct **digital circuits** or, synonymously, **gating networks.** The digital circuits (networks) are designed to perform some processing logic, for example, the addition of two binary input digits (A and B) with the resulting output digit C and the CARRY. This circuit can be constructed as follows.

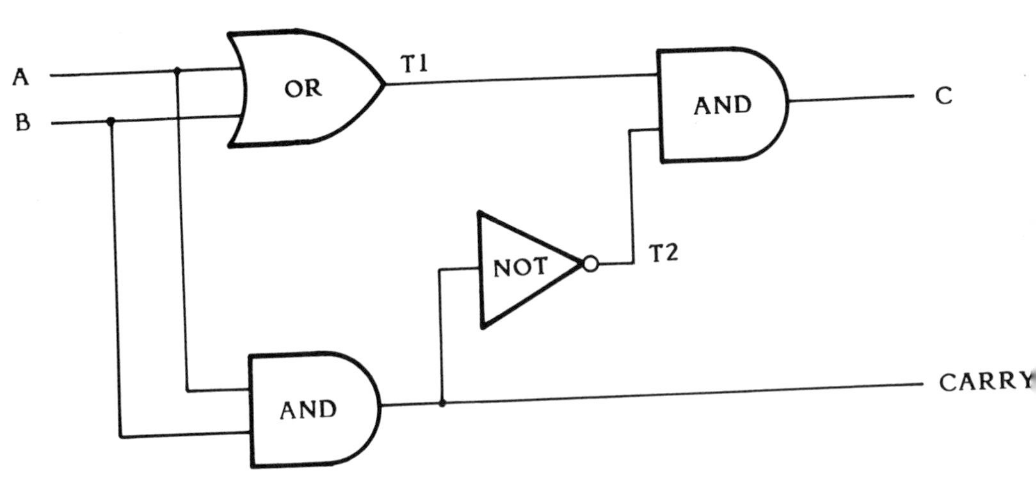

AN ADDER OF TWO BINARY DIGITS

This type of digital circuit which works on combinations of signals and gating processes is called a **combinational circuit.** Notice that the two input values A and B are sent to both the OR gate and the first AND gate at the same time; thus these two gating processes are executed as "parallel sequences." Next, the NOT gate is executed and finally the last AND gate is executed. Note that the CARRY was produced early in the circuit execution and the value of C at the latter part of the circuit execution. Thus, when signals are applied at the inputs A and B, further signals are generated as gate outputs. This generation of signals is called **signal propagation.** The total time that the circuit executes in producing its outputs is called the **propagation time** of the circuit. Propagation times for an adder circuit of this type are based upon the technology of the "transistors" used to realize the gates; however, in many modern technologies it can be as little as 2 to 3 nanoseconds (that is, 2 to 3 billionths of a second). The reason for the great speed of computer systems should now be obvious.

The logic of this adder circuit can also be represented in our dimensional flowchart process form as follows.

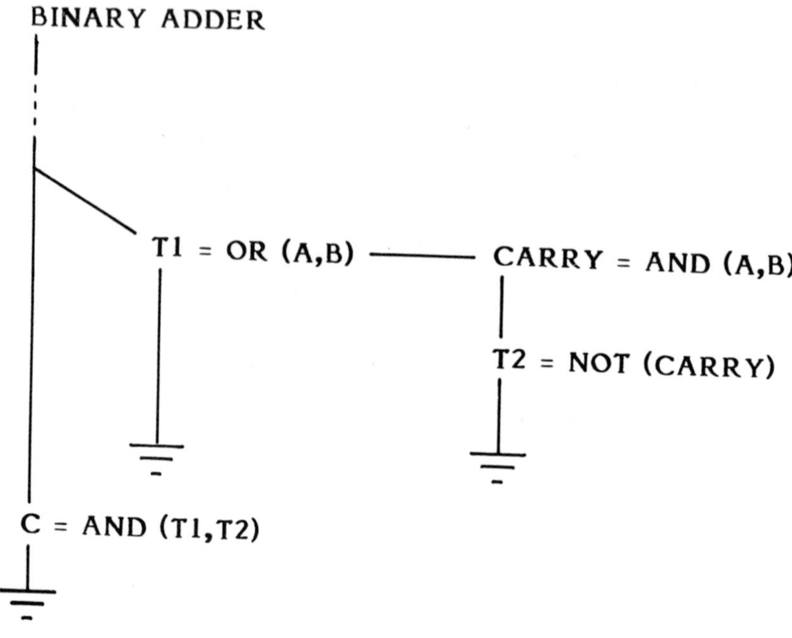
BINARY ADDER
T1 = OR (A,B)
CARRY = AND (A,B)
T2 = NOT (CARRY)
C = AND (T1,T2)

BINARY ADDER LOGIC

Here we note the use of intermediate signals labeled T1 and T2 as indicated in the previous picture. The use of the equal sign (=) in this context means that the signal to the left of the equal sign receives the output value of the named gate processes which have their inputs indicated in parenthesis. Note the use of "parallel sequence" execution of the logic sequences. Observe, however, that the NOT gate must be executed prior to the final AND gate. The reader should now as a human processor (using the circuit diagram and/or dimensional flowchart process) verify all of the combinations of binary values for A and B, namely (0, 0; 0, 1; 1, 0; and 1,1) and see that the results agree with the earlier provided binary digit additions.

It is important to observe that in the building of this digital circuit, we have created a new digital process which is composed of gate processes. We have indeed built a higher level process. This is the beginning of the construction of many "higher level processes" that will go all the way up to the end "users" of the computer system. This building of processes upon processes will be further illuminated in the following chapter. The important thing to remember at this point is, as stated earlier, "one man's processes are another man's processor".

The adder of two binary digits that we have illustrated is called a **half adder.** A half adder is a basic process that is used in a so-called **full adder;** that is, an adder process which, in addition to the logic of a half adder, includes the logic to take account of carries from other adder circuits. There are basically two strategies used for the adders in computer systems which correspond to our notions of serial contra parallel transmission as presented in chapter 6: namely, **serial adders** which add one digit from each input value during a time frame including carry logic and **parallel adders** which add all digits of the two values during the same time frame (including carry adjustments). The parallel adder has a half adder for the least significant binary digit and then full adders which include carry logic for all the higher order binary digits. Parallel adders are normally designed to deal with a fixed number of binary digits of precision (ex. 2, 4, 8, 12, 16, 24, 32, 36 or 64 bits). Parallel adders are obviously faster than serial adders. It is possible to build parallel adders today for anywhere from 2 to 64 bits of precision that have a "propagation time" of no more than 6-8 nanoseconds (that is, 6 to 8 billionths of a second). "Try to beat that with your paper and pencil."

In the previous chapter, we introduced flip/flops (latches) as memory elements that retain their states while power is supplied to the computer system. A flip/flop is realized via the use of gate processes. However, we should first mention that there are two additional gate processes which are basic building blocks of logic design; namely, the **NAND gate** and the **NOR gate** which are represented as follows.

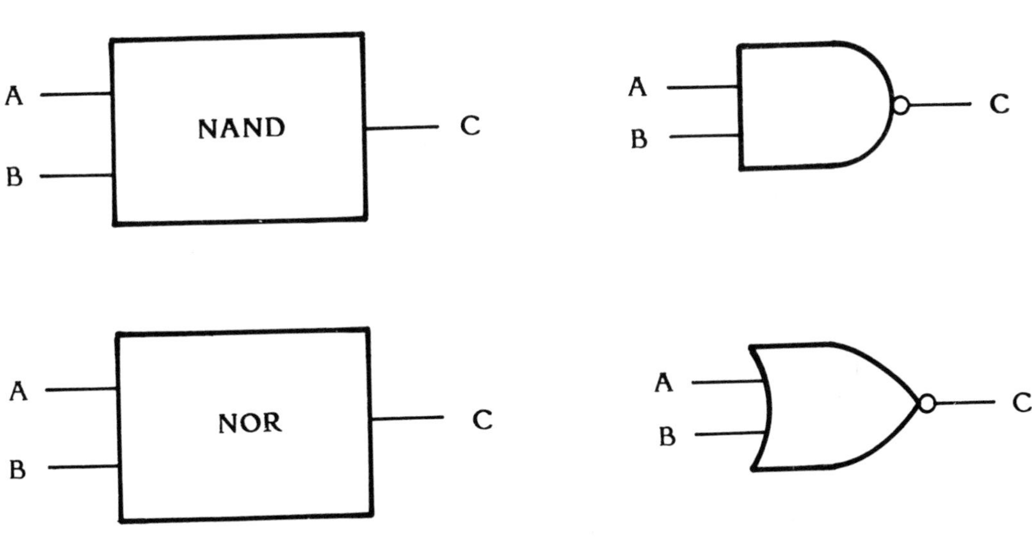

ADDITIONAL BASIC DIGITAL PROCESSES

These gates are simply combinations of the use of an AND gate or an OR gate, followed by a NOT gate. Thus, they are single gate processes which are equivalent to the following simple digital circuits (gating networks).

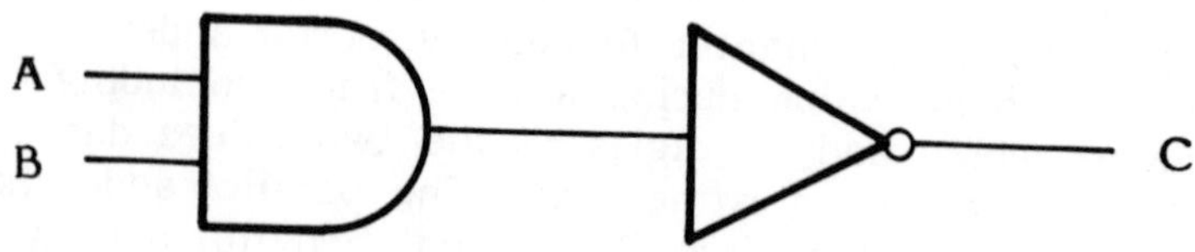

CIRCUIT EQUIVALENT TO THE NAND GATE

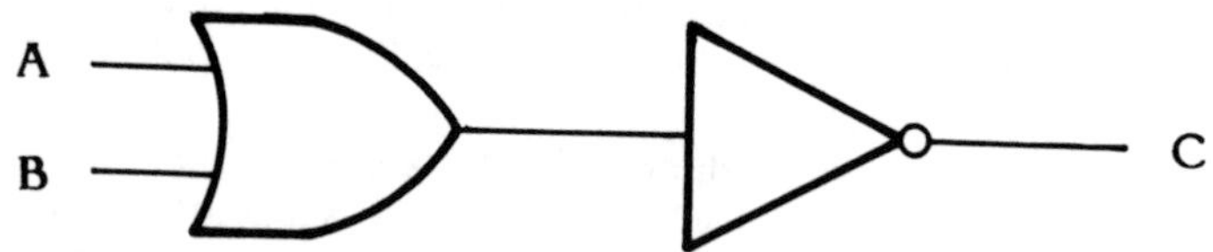

CIRCUIT EQUIVALENT TO THE NOR GATE

As with the AND, OR and NOT gates, we can easily develop a complete enumeration of all possible inputs and outputs of these two gates as follows.

	SIGNAL VALUES		
GATE	A	B	C
NAND	0	0	1
	0	1	1
	1	0	1
	1	1	0
NOR	0	0	1
	0	1	0
	1	0	0
	1	1	0

The reader should compare this enumeration with the earlier enumeration of the AND and OR gates and observe that in all cases, the output C is simply the complement (opposite value) of the AND and OR gate results for C. Verify these new gate functions by passing all possible values of A and B through the circuit equivalent given in the previous picture. **Important:** Our list of gate processes is now complete. This is the entire set used for logic design of all possible digital circuits. Returning to the flip/flop, we shall now consider how a digital circuit is utilized to provide a flip/flop process. A possible circuit is as follows.

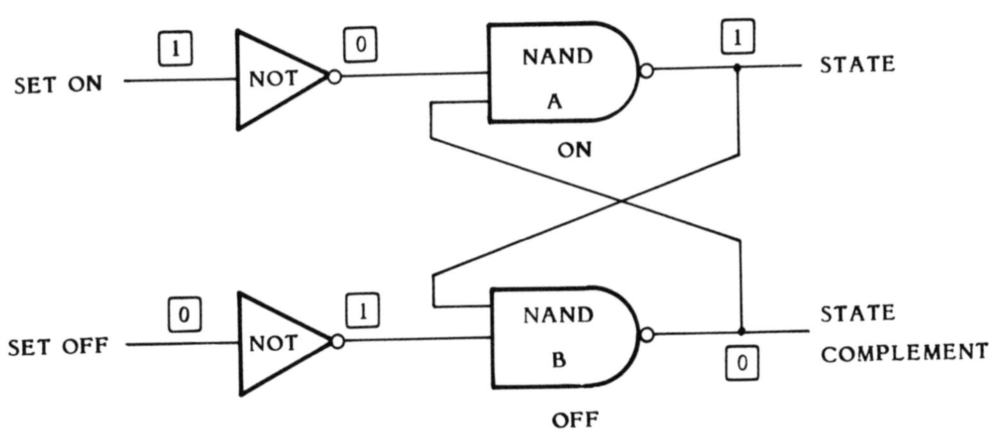

FLIP/FLOP CIRCUIT DIAGRAM

The values in boxes represent the signal values where 1 is for high voltage (for example +2 volts) and 0 is for low voltage (for example 0 volts). You will observe that when the SET ON line is 1, its complement, given by the NOT gate, is 0 and is one input to NAND gate A; the other input must also be 0 if NAND gate A is to give a 1 as the STATE of the flip/flop. This is assured in this case by the SET OFF line being 0 resulting in a complement of 1 via the NOT gate and thus causing NAND gate B to have a 0 result as the STATE COMPLEMENT of the flip/flop. Note the coupling of the output of each NAND gate back into the other NAND gate as an input. The reader should verify what happens when SET ON goes to 0 and SET OFF goes to 1.

The clock signal used to specify "when" the flip/flop value is to be changed has not been illustrated. However, this is accomplished by using two AND gates prior to the two NOT gates in which the clock signal and the respective SET ON, SET OFF signals are inputs to the respective AND gates. The reader should, as an exercise, redraw the entire gating network to include this part that was not provided. The approach used to realizing the flip/flop process here is only one approach. It is possible to use other gating network circuits which provide the equivalent flip/flop process function.

As mentioned in the previous chapter, arrays of flip/flops (latches) are used to build registers or memory cells. In "combinational circuits" as demonstrated earlier, there are no memory elements. The output values are available as long as the signals are applied at the inputs, subject to propagation time when an input signal changes. Flip/flops on the other hand have the ability to retain the state ON or OFF as long as power is supplied. Flip/flop elements are an important part of the second major form of digital circiut: namely the **sequential circuit** which combines a memory element (one or more flip/flops, perhaps a register or even a larger memory array) and a combinational circuit as indicated in the following.

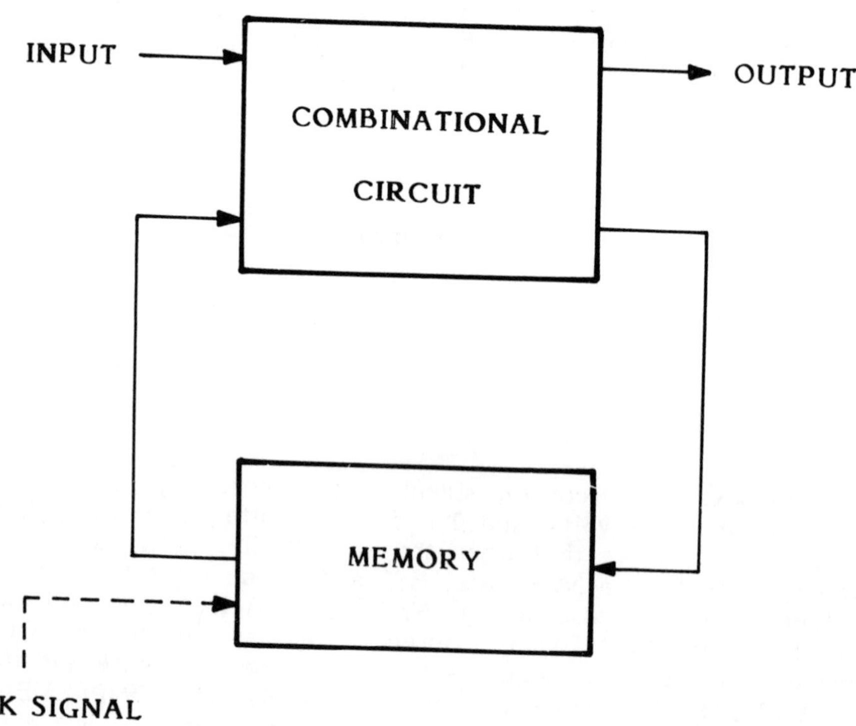

A SEQUENTIAL CIRCUIT

The word sequential should be taken to mean that things happen in sequence one after another (like our discussion of the processing of the records of sequential files in chapter 8). The clock signal determines when things will happen. For example, at the time of the clock signal, the current state of all or part of the memory flip/flops may be "read out" along with a new input and delivered to the gates of the combinational circuit for execution. After propagation through this gating network, at the next marking of the clock signal, the results are stored back into all or some of the flip/flops in the memory and outputs "may" be produced.

The reader can easily visualize, for example, that a value to be added to a register as input and the register as a flip/flop memory are both delivered to a parallel adder (the combinational circuit) which adds these binary values; and then at the next clock marking, the result is stored back into the flip/flops of a register. Many processes in computer systems are realized in precisely this manner. A sequential circuit is the lowest level of "finite state machine" in computer systems. The state transitions occur at the time of a clock signal when the results are stored back into the memory. "Previous states" as well as new inputs are taken into account in generating the "next states" and possible outputs.

The final subject of our discussion of digital circuits is the question of the **timing sequence** as provided by a clock signal. The reader has undoubtedly observed that it is the clock signal which is the true "driver" of digital processes. The clock signal controls when things will happen. In digital processes, clock signals are generated as an "oscillating" signal. That is, the value of the signal alternates between high and low voltage levels as indicated in the following picture.

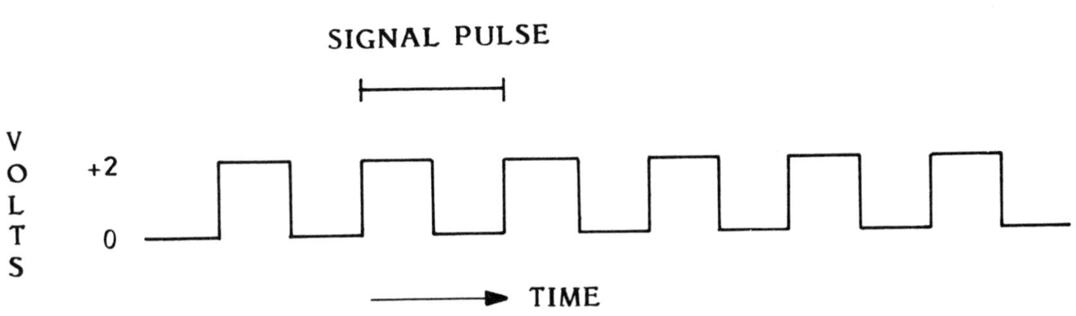

THE OSCILLATIONS OF A CLOCK SIGNAL

Again we use 0 volts and +2 volts to illustrate low and high voltages. This form of signal, in general, is called a **square edge signal** where each individual oscillation is called a **signal pulse.** When the pulse rises to high voltage, we call this the **leading edge** of the pulse and when it is descending we call it the **trailing edge.**

The clock signal is delivered to the sequential circuits of the cooperating hardware processes where normal AND and NAND gates are used to determine the starting and ending points of logic execution within the circuit. In sequential circuits, for example, input values and memory values are delivered to the combinational circuit at the "leading edge" of a clock pulse and results must be propogated ("produced") for storing into the memory and outputs produced at the time of the next leading edge pulse.

The rate of oscillation of the clock pulse determines the performance of the hardware logic. However, the logic must be designed so that all necessary propagations within the circuits activated at the leading edge are completed before the next leading edge. Note that this is precisely the phenomenon we described in chapter 4 under the discussion of synchronous control. The faster circuits are forced to wait upon the slowest of circuits (the worst case).

The Packaging of Gates and Circuits

We have now considered the basic digital processes (gates) and their use in the construction of more advanced processes, namely digital circuits (gating networks). In modern electronic technology, gates are realized by transistors and the transistors of several gates and their connecting signal paths are packaged in **integrated circuits.** The number of gates placed into an integrated circuit is utilized to categorize the degree of integration as follows.

Small Scale Integration (SSI)	1 to 10 gates
Medium Scale Integration (MSI)	hundreds of gates
Large Scale Integration (LSI)	thousands of gates
Very Large Scale Integration (VLSI)	over 100,000 gates

The integrated circuit technology advanced extremely fast during the 1970's and has lead to LSI and VLSI components which can include entire central processing units, extremely large flip/flop memories (semi-conductor memories as mentioned earlier) and other advanced highly integrated processes. The 1970's were the age of the **microprocessor** when the computing field changed its character from being based upon the availability of only large expensive computer systems to the availability of small inexpensive computer systems.

The reader may now ask: How is an integrated circuit built and what does it look like? The transistors and connections of integrated circuits are placed onto a substance called a **wafer,** usually by photographic means. The source for the photographic process is a picture of the transistors and connections of the circuit called the **mask.** In fact many copies of the circuit mask are placed onto the wafer which appears as indicated in the following picture.

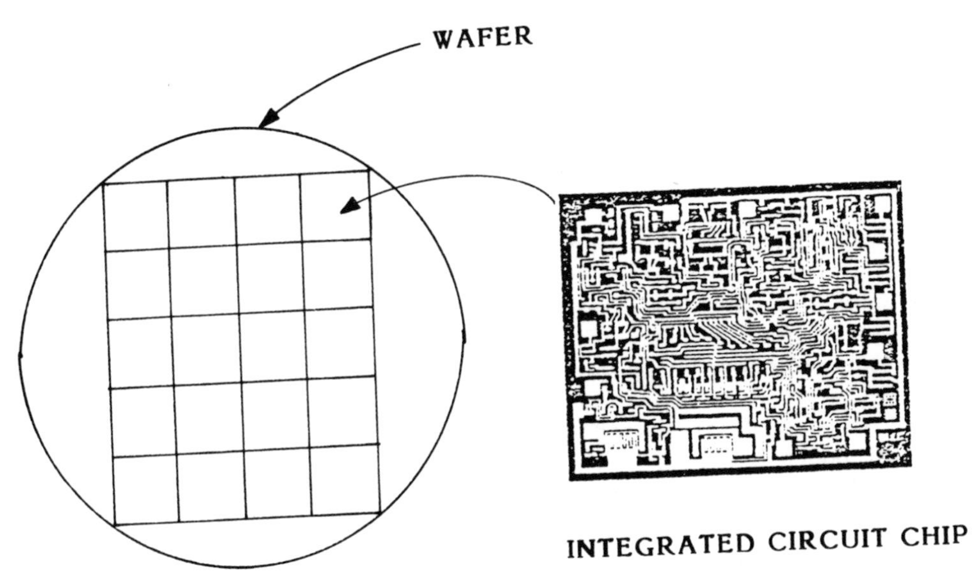

INTEGRATED CIRCUIT FABRICATION

Each individual integrated circuit is called a **chip.** The material used for the wafer as well as the photographic process used to realize the integrated circuit can vary and thus several technologies for fabrication have evolved. The density of transistors permitted per chip and the circuit propagation times vary based upon the selected technology. The following is an enumeration of some of the prevalent technologies:

Transistor-Transistor Logic (TTL)
Metallic Oxide Semiconductor (MOS)
Silicon On Sapphire (SOS)
Integrated Injection Logic (I2L) pronounced (I-squared-L)
Emitter Coupled Logic (ECL)

When the wafer is produced, the chips are tested by an automatic testing device and only "good" chips are selected for use. The good chips are then broken away from the wafer by a cutting device and are mounted into a capsule called a **Dual In-Line Package** (DIP), which is illustrated as follows.

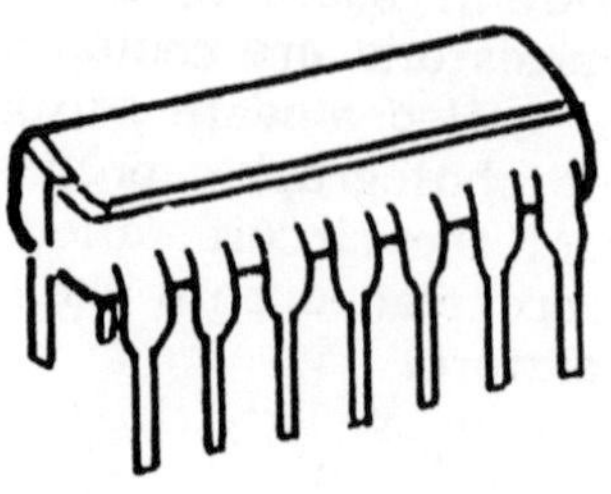

DUAL IN-LINE PACKAGE (DIP)

The word "dual" comes from the fact that there are two rows of **pins** which provide the "ports" for the DIP process input and output signals. Inside of the DIP, the integrated circuit is connected to the pins by extremely small wires. The DIP is now a process ready for inclusion in a system of cooperating processes.

In most uses of integrated circuits, the DIPs are mounted onto a **printed circuit board** (PC-board) which contains signals connecting the DIPs as illustrated in the following picture.

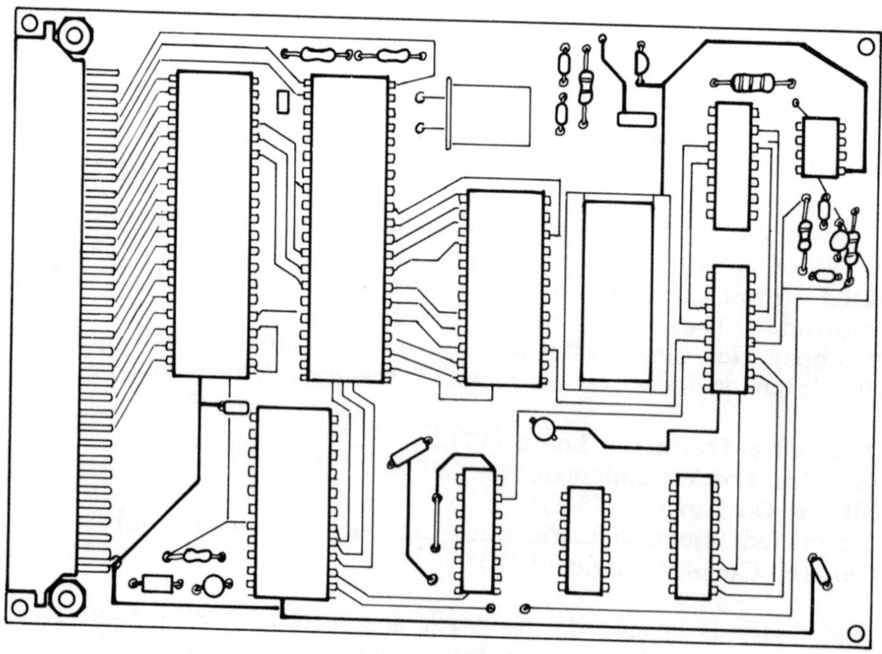

PRINTED CIRCUIT BOARD (PC-BOARD)

The "ports" of the printed circuit board used for receiving and sending signals are located at the edges and are called **edge connectors.** Printed circuit boards may then be incorporated as processes into a more advanced system of cooperating processes. However a single PC-board may well contain a complete computer system, including the processors for the memory, Central Processing Unit and Input/Output Controller processes and the buses (highways) that connect these processes. The peripheral devices are then connected by **cables** to the edge connectors. Some of the edge connectors are used for attaching power cables to the PC-board where the power is provided by a **power supply.** The power is distributed over the PC-board to the integrated circuit components.

In larger computer systems, the hardware logic and memories may be distributed over several PC-boards, each with their own edge connectors used for power contacts with a power supply and connections with related processes contained on neighboring PC-boards. In this case, the PC-boards are placed in a **chassis,** synonymously called a **rack.** One or more I/O channels are connected to appropriate PC-board processes in the Input/Output controller logic. One or more peripheral devices may be connected to each I/O channel. These construction concepts are illustrated in the following picture.

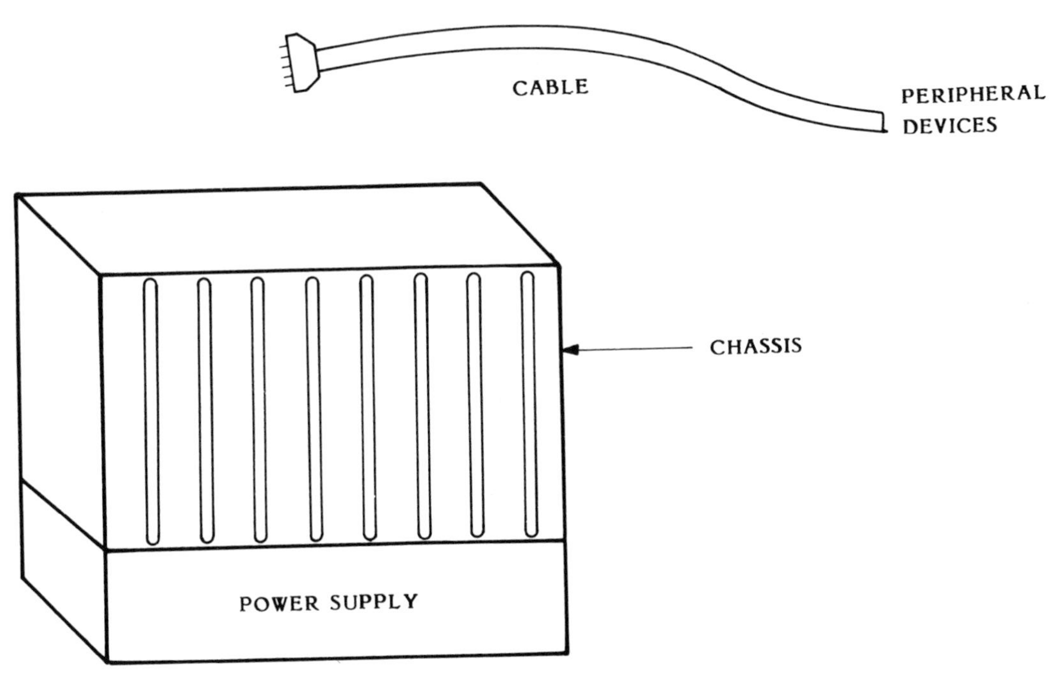

A MULTI PC-BOARD COMPUTER SYSTEM

In all computer system applications, the computer system is only a process of a larger system of cooperating processes. This is very obvious in process control applications. In this environment, the **single board computer** has revolutionized process control design. Further, single board computers are small enough to be included in a typewriter and this has enabled the development of inexpensive "word processing systems" as presented in chapter 6. It is said that, in the future, all typewriters produced will be equipped with a computer system.

The reader has now been introduced to the non-trivial world of digital logic design and the creation of digital processes which are the foundation stones of computer systems. For those who shall specialize in a computer systems profession, this discussion will have provided an important platform; whereas, the layreader will have a good idea of what lies at the bottom of computer technology.

Summary

The most basic of the digital processes are called **gates** which form the basis for digital **logic design.** The **AND gate,** the **OR gate** and the **NOT gate** are the three basic gate processes. These three gates correspond to the operations of the **Boolean algebra** which is the basis for realizing computer arithmetic. Combinations of gates that process signals are called **digital circuits,** or **gating networks.** The basic circuit type is called a **combinational circuit.** The movement of signals through a digital circuit is called **signal propagation** and the time taken for the circuit to produce its output signals is called its **propagation time.**

An important process constructed as a combination of the basic gate processes is the **half adder** which adds two binary digital values and produces an output digit and carry digit. A **full adder** includes half adder logic plus the logic to accomodate carries. A computer system adder that processes one binary digit of arithmetic at a time is called a **serial adder;** whereas, a **parallel adder** operates on all binary digits of the given precision simultaneously.

Above the three basic gating processes, there exist two further processes which are, in reality, simply combinations of AND or OR gates, with a NOT gate. These gates are called the **NAND gate** and the **NOR gate.** The use of a digital circuit for realizing a flip/flop process was illustrated. A more advanced form of digital circuit that contains a combinational circuit and a memory is the **sequential circuit** which is the most primitive form of a "finite state machine."

The driving force that controls activities in digital circuits is the **timing sequence** provided by a clock signal. The oscillating voltages of the clock signal give it the form of a **square edge signal** where each oscillation is called a **signal pulse.** The signal pulse is divided into a **leading edge** when the signal rises and a **trailing edge** when the signal falls. The logic of the activated combinational and sequential circuits must be completed between successive leading edges.

Gates are realized via transistors which are packaged into **integrated circuits.** Integrated circuits are categorized according to the degree of integration and the following terms have evolved: **Small Scale Integration** (SSI), **Medium Scale Integration** (MSI), **Large Scale Integration** (LSI) and **Very Large Scale Integration** (VLSI). One of the major accomplishments of the 1970's made possible by large scale integration was the introduction of the **microprocessor.**

Integrated circuits are fabricated on **wafers** by using a photographic process involving a **mask** drawing which indicates the transistors for gates and their connections. Several materials have been used for wafers as well as several variations of photographic processes. Some of the best known technologies are as follows: **Transistor-Transistor Logic** (TTL), **Metallic Oxide Semiconductor** (MOS), **Silicon on Sapphire** (SOS), **Integrated Injection Logic** (I2L) pronounced (I-squared-L) and **Emitter Coupled Logic** (ECL). Many integrated circuit **chips** are photographed onto the wafer, but only good chips are cut out of the wafer for placement in a **Dual In-Line Package** (DIP).

The integrated circuit is attached to **pins** of the DIP by wires. DIP's normally are mounted as cooperating processes on a **printed circuit board (PC-board)** which has **edge connectors** for its input and output signal ports. When a single PC-board contains a CPU, memory and I/O controller, some of the edge connectors are used for the connecting of the **cables** of the I/O channels. Further edge connectors are used for supplying power from a **power supply.** When more than one PC-board is required, the PC-boards are mounted into a **chassis,** also called a **rack.** The availability of so-called **single board computers** has permitted the convenient incorporation of computers into other larger systems, for example, in process control systems or in a typewriter thus providing an inexpensive word processing system.

Word List

The basic principles of computer hardware have been presented in this chapter. Readers should verify their knowledge of the concepts and terminology presented in the chapter by reviewing the following terms.

- gates
- logic design
- AND gate
- OR gate
- NOT gate
- Boolean algebra
- digital circuits
- gating networks
- combinational circuit
- signal propagation
- propagation time
- half adder
- full adder
- serial adder
- parallel adder
- NAND gate
- NOR gate
- sequential circuit
- timing sequence
- square edge signal
- signal pulse
- leading edge
- trailing edge
- integrated circuits
- SSI
- MSI
- LSI
- VLSI
- microprocessor
- wafer
- mask
- TTL
- MOS
- SOS
- I2L (I-squared-L)
- ECL
- chip
- Dual In-Line Package (DIP)
- pins
- printed circuit board
- edge connectors
- cables
- power supply
- chassis (rack)
- single board computers

Problems

1. Perform binary addition on the following binary values. Indicate the decimal equivalent of each input value and the result.

0000	0000	0110	1111	1010	1111
+0000	+1111	+1001	+0001	+1010	+1111
____	____	____	____	____	____

2. Construct dimensional flowchart logic for the NAND and NOR gate processes in the same manner as provided for the AND, OR and NOT gates.

3. An important combinational circuit is a "comparator" which determines if two binary input values are equal (i.e. both binary 0's or both binary 1's). Draw a digital circuit (gating network) which compares two binary digits A and B resulting in a binary 1 if they are equal or a binary 0 if they are not equal. Hint: use AND and NAND gates plus an OR gate.

4. Construct a gating network for a comparator that compares 4 digits of two binary values, namely A1:B1, A2:B2, A3:B3 and A4:B4. Use the values given in problem (1) in order to test your digital circuit. Further, draw a dimensional flowchart which shows the parallel sequences that can be utilized in this circuit.

Chapter 10
THE "ARCHITECTURE" OF COMPUTER SYSTEMS

In the previous four chapters, we have considered the data processed by computer systems, the cooperating processes (namely, memory, Central Processing Unit, Input/Output controller and peripheral devices) and the basic digital "hardware" processes from which processors are constructed. There are many alternative strategies to be evaluated and decisions to be made in the design and construction of computer systems. These decisions are based largely upon the intended "end use" of the computer systems. This "architectural" aspect of computer systems is highly related to architecture in general as noted in the following quotation.

> "COMPUTER ARCHITECTURE, LIKE OTHER ARCHITECTURE, IS THE **ART OF DETERMINING THE NEEDS OF THE USER** OF A STRUCTURE AND THEN DESIGNING TO MEET THESE NEEDS AS EFFECTIVELY AS POSSIBLE WITHIN ECONOMIC AND TECHNICAL CONSTRAINTS. ARCHITECTURE MUST INCLUDE ENGINEERING CONSIDERATIONS, SO THAT THE DESIGN WILL BE ECONOMICAL AND FEASIBLE; BUT THE EMPHASIS IN ARCHITECTURE IS UPON THE NEEDS OF THE USER, WHEREAS IN ENGINEERING THE EMPHASIS IS UPON THE NEEDS OF THE FABRICATOR."
>
> FREDRICK P. BROOKS, JR.

Note that the needs of the "user" are emphasized. Computer systems may be designed to meet the rather narrow needs of a small group of users and therefore are called **special purpose systems;** whereas, computer systems that are designed to meet the needs of a large diverse group of users are called **general purpose systems.** The reader may quickly draw the analogy to the architecture of buildings, for example, buildings designed for special purpose use (as, swimming halls) and those designed for general purpose use (meeting halls). In the previous chapter, we dealt with the low level building block processes that are used in constructing higher level processes and noted that **"one person's processes are another person's processor."** In the computer systems milieu there is a hierarchy of various types of skills utilized in creating processors from more basic processes as indicated in the picture on the following page.

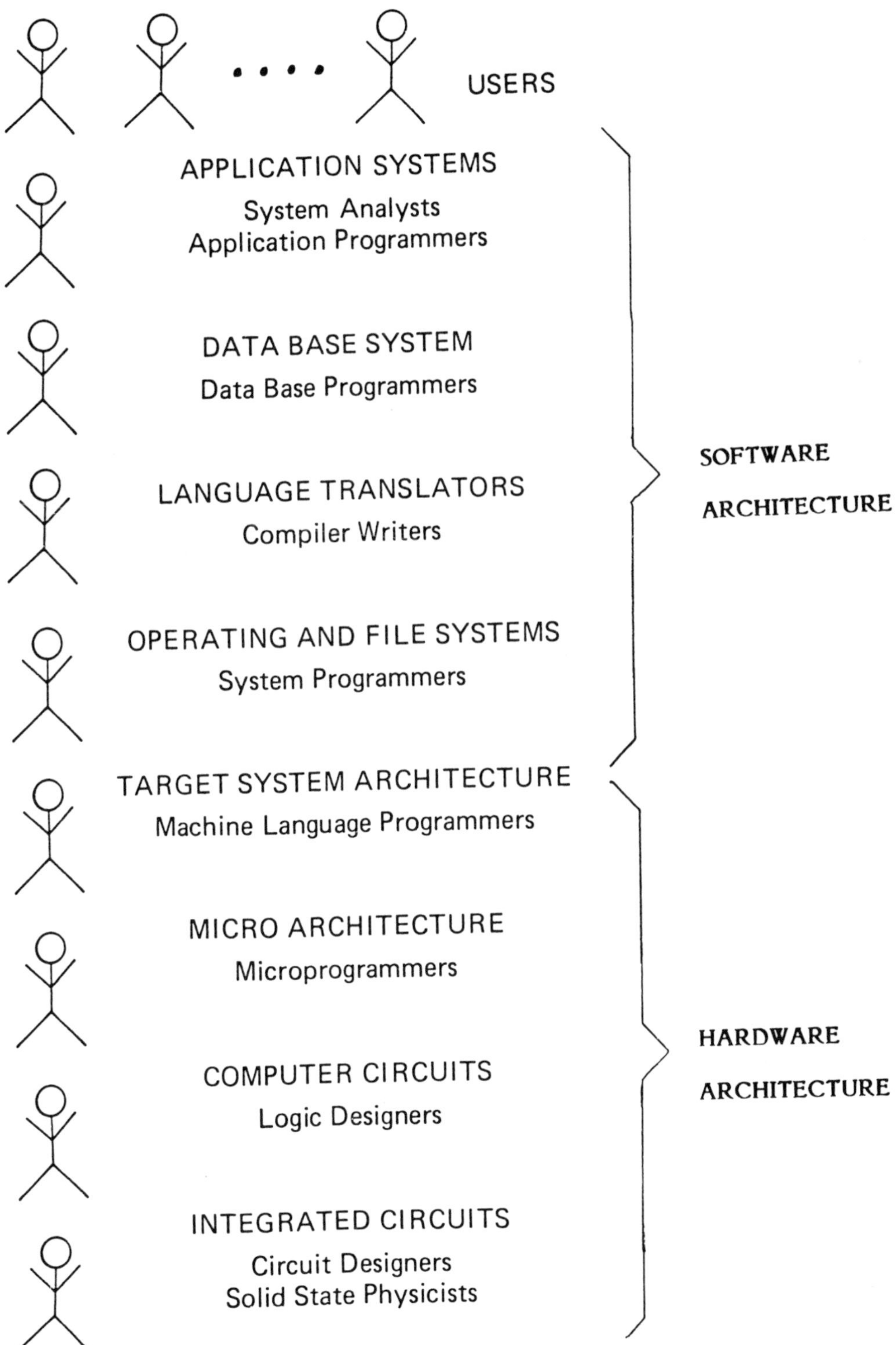
USERS
APPLICATION SYSTEMS
System Analysts
Application Programmers
DATA BASE SYSTEM
Data Base Programmers
LANGUAGE TRANSLATORS
Compiler Writers
OPERATING AND FILE SYSTEMS
System Programmers
TARGET SYSTEM ARCHITECTURE
Machine Language Programmers
MICRO ARCHITECTURE
Microprogrammers
COMPUTER CIRCUITS
Logic Designers
INTEGRATED CIRCUITS
Circuit Designers
Solid State Physicists
SOFTWARE
ARCHITECTURE
HARDWARE
ARCHITECTURE

This picture illustrates an important point; namely, that **computer systems are designed and constructed by people.** Over the brief history of computer systems, several new job categories have evolved and the reader will undoubtedly recognize the names given to several of these professions. All of the people above the integrated circuit level use lower level processes in their efforts to produce higher level processors. Consequently, we have several "levels of users" and therefore we have several "sub-architectures". We can apply Brook's comments about computer architecture to each sub-architecture. At every coupling of groups of specialists, one faces the decision of the degree of the general purposeness versus the degree of special purposeness of the processes provided as the building blocks for the next higher level. Designers and implementors at all levels must be conscious of the use to which their processes will be applied on higher levels.

In designing effective computer systems, the computer architect has many aspects to consider since all of the sub-architectural levels represent building blocks upon which the "total architecture" must be based. The computer architect has the responsibility of distributing the activities and desired properties of the computer systems structure to these various hardware and software levels of the computer system. The computer architect therefore must be acquainted with the structure and composition, possibilities and limitations of hardware processes and of "programmed processes," namely, the computer software structure. We shall now consider some additional properties of programmed processes over and above those already presented in earlier chapters.

Further Properties of Programming

A large majority of the processes of a computer system are, in fact, programmed processes. Further, as we can see from the previous picture, there are many different levels of programming activities involved in providing usable computer systems. In reality, all levels, with the exception of the solid state physics of integrated circuits, involve programming. The "programs" of the process logic of integrated circuits and digital processes are programs created once, at the time of their design and construction and are not changed; that is, they are **static programmed processes.** On the other hand, programs that are placed temporarily into a memory process and used to control the activities of a processor (Central Processing Unit) in realizing a higher level process are **dynamic programmed processes** created by the translation of a source program and "executed" from the memory process. The reader will remember the assembly language program of chapter 7 which provides an example of process logic.

While the details of the types of programming performed at the various levels vary, there are many general principles of program structure which are common across the levels. The basic notions of "sequence," "selection," "refinement" and "repetitive sequence" as introduced in chapter 5, plus the notion of "parallel sequences" as indicated in chapter

9, are constructs that are used in all types of programming. In previous examples of programmed processes, we have implied that the procedures of the process are activated in response to some external "event" happening (as, initial or start signal) resulting in the initiation of the procedure execution. The notion of a procedure is a more general concept in the world of programming. Procedures are an organizational unit which carry out some well structured logical activity and, in addition to perhaps being executed as a result of an event happening, **procedures may utilize the logic of other procedures.** In this respect it is a type of **dynamic refinement** as opposed to our earlier notion of refinement where all procedure logic was incorporated statically inside the procedure. One procedure can call upon ("invoke") another procedure. When this **procedure invocation** occurs, the logic of the called procedure is, in effect, dynamically coupled in as a refinement of the calling procedure. The general principles behind this idea are illustrated in the following picture.

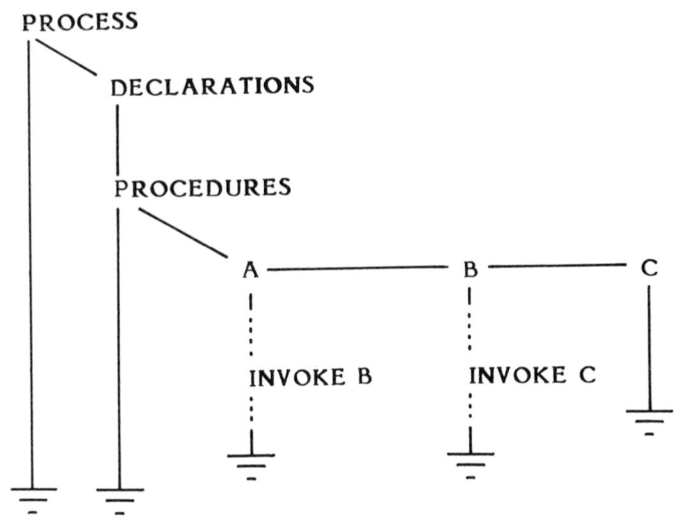

PROCEDURE (SUBROUTINE) STRUCTURE

As noted in the picture, a synonymous word for procedure and one that is well recognized in the programming community is the term **subroutine.** Here we see that in procedure A, we invoke (call upon) procedure B. This invocation means that all of the logic of procedure B is coupled in dynamically as a refinement at the point of the invocation from procedure A. Likewise, in the execution of procedure B, the invocation of procedure C couples in the logic of procedure C at this point. At the completion of procedure C, control is returned to procedure B for the completion of the logic of procedure B and at the completion of procedure B control returns to procedure A for the completion of the logic of procedure A. This dynamic refinement is illustrated in the following picture.

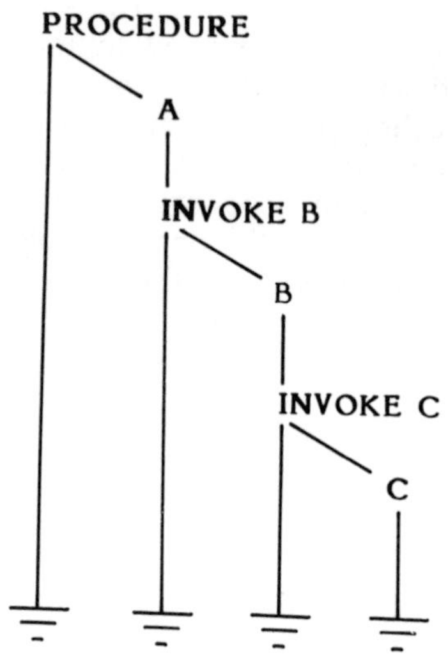

DYNAMIC REFINEMENT OF
PROCEDURE (SUBROUTINE) EXECUTION

We can see that the effect of invocation is the coupling of the logic of the called procedure (subroutine) into the calling procedure as a refinement. This coupling exists only as long as the called procedure is executing; when it is completed and control returns to the calling procedure, the dynamic refinement disappears. Instructions are provided at the machine language level for making calls upon procedures (subroutines) and for returning from called procedures (subroutines). Let us now consider these additions to the basic types of machine language instructions that were presented in chapter 7.

Procedure Control Instructions permit the construction and utilization of procedures (subroutines).

Operation Code Field	Operand Field
CALL	Memory Address
RETURN	

The call instruction specifies the memory address of the first instruction of the procedure (subroutine) to be invoked. The CPU, in a working register of its local state, retains the memory address of the instruction following the call instruction for later use when "returning" from the called procedure (subroutine). Procedure execution starts by placing the address of the first instruction of the procedure in the PROGRAM LOCATION COUNTER and continues until a return instruction is executed, at which point the memory address retained in the working register at the time of the "calling" is placed into the PROGRAM LOCATION COUNTER. Thus execution resumes at the instruction located after the call instruction.

The use of these two additional machine language instructions will be illustrated later in the chapter.

As mentioned several times, there are many levels of programmed processes in computer systems. The programs of the processes which are contained in the memory process must be "interpreted" by some processor that understands the language of the programs. In order to gain a conceptual understanding of the many levels of programmed processes, we shall consider the structure of **processor-memory pairs,** that is, the place where the process programs and state variables (data) are stored (the memory) and the processor which is the program interpreter as illustrated in the following picture.

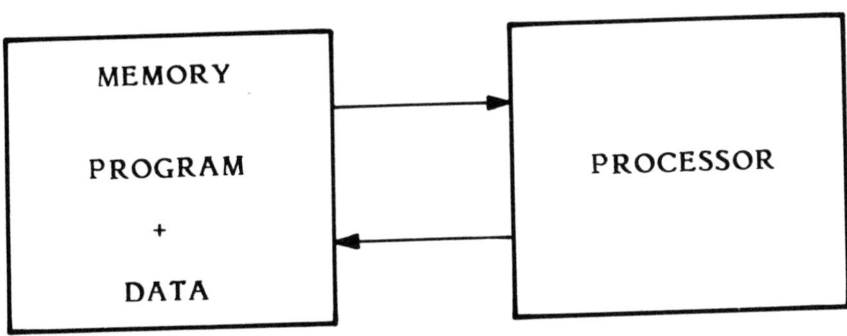

PROCESSOR-MEMORY PAIR

THE BASIS FOR CONSTRUCTING PROGRAMMED PROCESSES

Many programmed processes can be contained in the same processor-memory pair in the form of machine language programs and data areas (one or more memory cells) for their respective state variables. They "share" the available memory space. This **memory sharing** will be vividly demonstrated in the following sections.

The Architecture of the Target System

The term **target system** is synonymous with our earlier notion of the machine language level as presented in chapter 7. It is the basic processor-memory pair that is used for the further building of the software programmed processes and, as indicated in the first picture of this chapter, it is the boundary between the hardware and software architectures. In this case, the processor is equivalent to the Central Processing Unit (CPU). The architecture of a modern target system is represented as "nested" processor-memory pairs in the following picture.

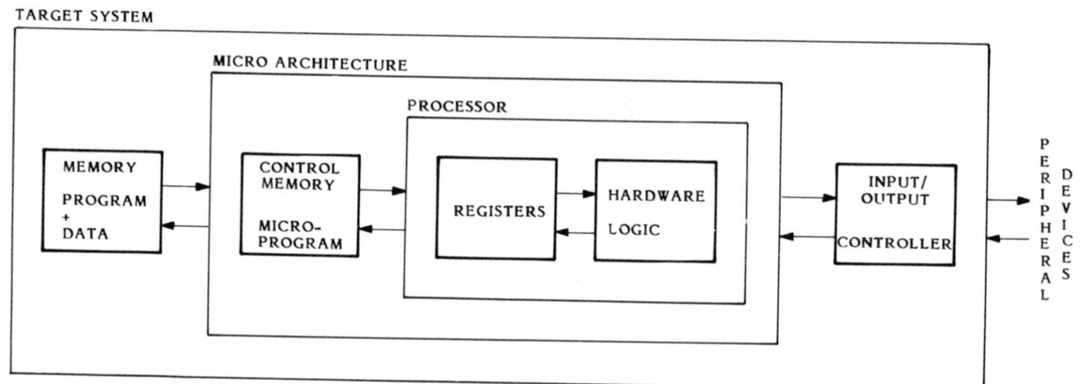

ARCHITECTURE OF THE TARGET SYSTEM

The enclosures here identify the various levels of the sub-architecture. Let us first consider the innermost processor. The hardware logic is the basic digital processes composed of combinational and sequential circuits (including local memories, namely, registers and other state variable objects). In early computer systems, processors of this variety were utilized to directly interpret the machine language of the computer. However, in the early 1950's (*) the notion of utilizing another level of architecture, that is, a **micro architecture** evolved.

With the introduction of micro architecture, the hardware logic became "programmed" with a new type of program called the **microprogram** which

(*) The concept of a micro architecture and microprogramming was first introduced in 1951 by Professor Maurice Wilkes of Cambridge University, England.

is contained in a **control memory.** In this case, the hardware processor interprets the **microinstructions** coming from the control memory which tells it which type of operations to perform in the hardware logic. These operations include the transfers of data between registers and other state variables, etc. The languages for microprogramming have often been referred to as **register transfer languages.**

The microprogram controls communication with the Input/Output controller as indicated in the picture. The microprogram is also used to control the target system fetching of program instructions (machine language instructions) and data from the target system memory. The use of the micro architecture and the microprogram provides the identity of the target system; namely the machine language level. In the late 1960's and during the 1970's the development of micro architectures made rather major advances and it is today the predominant means of Central Processing Unit design and construction. As a result of these advances, micro architectures which were always special purpose systems for aiding in constructing a single target system architecture can be designed to be more general purpose. Thus, one can think of utilizing the same micro architecture and, through the provision of various microprograms, creating processors for various target systems while utilizing the same basic processor hardware structure. However, the major advantage of utilizing a micro architecture (which was the original reason) is to reduce the complexity of hardware logic. Without the utilization of a micro architecture, a large number of complex combinational and sequential circuits are required in order to build a processor. By deciding to program a simpler processor containing fewer combinational and sequential circuits we obtain a more consistent and understandable structure of the target system architecture. The following point of view helps to clarify the organizational aspects of a micro architecture.

> "MICROPROGRAMMING IS AN EXTENSION OF THE SUBROUTINE CONCEPT DOWN TO A LEVEL WHICH PREVIOUSLY WAS HIDDEN TO THE PROGRAMMER".
>
> PER-ERIK DANIELSSON

The target system architecture provided by these low level procedures (subroutines) for machine language interpretation forms the basis for building higher level programmed processes which is the part referred to as the software architecture. The target system memory will be shared amongst these higher level software processes.

Operating and File Systems

A naked target system is not of much use without an effective software system built upon it. We must build up supporting software processes with procedures that provide basic services so that all "users" of the target system **do not have to redesign and reprogram, over and over again,** the same basic software processes. The first level of software systems built upon target systems are usually the so-called **operating system** and **file system** as indicated in the following picture.

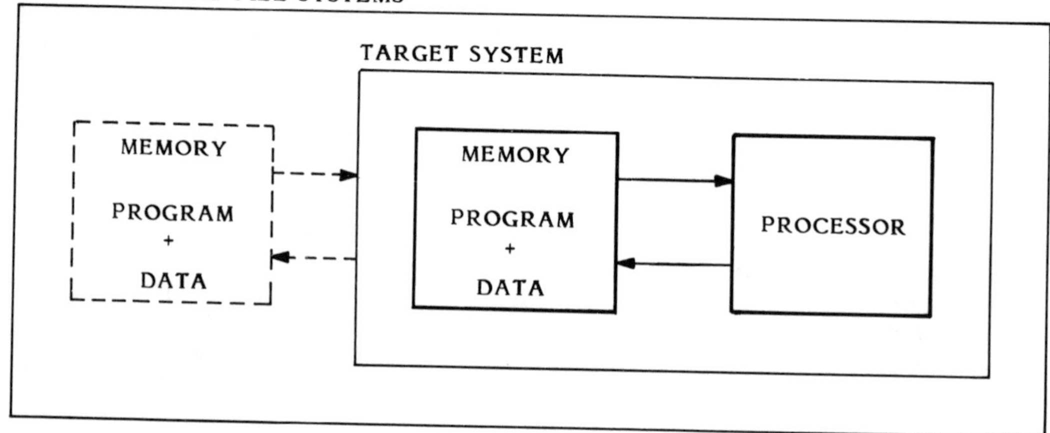

OPERATING AND FILE SYSTEMS

We note here that the processor-memory pair target system forms a higher level processor which is coupled as a part of a higher level processor-memory pair, to a memory indicated in dotted lines. In this case, we utilize this dotted notation to indicate that this is **not** a new physical memory, but is the target system memory. In fact, the operating and/or file systems use only a portion of the physical target system memory for their operation. The physical memory is shared amongst software systems.

File systems are built to manage the details of the processing of "sequential" and "random access" files as described in chapter 8. The detailed programming required for controlling storage peripheral devices is quite complicated and these processes of the file system provide us with a higher level of "file processor" that we can utilize in constructing higher level processes. The services of the file processor includes the cataloging of files by their **file names** in a **file directory.** The file directory, as well as the files themselves, are stored on the media of the storage peripherals (ex. tapes or discs). The file processor provides the service of managing the creation, modification and deletion of individual files.

The operating system is a manager of the resources of the computer system. It provides controlled access to the resources, namely, memory, Central Processing Unit (CPU) and input/output facilities. It permits the sharing of these resources amongst the active software systems which are composed of processes recognized by the target system processor including the operating system itself. In this role, it utilizes the concept of "monitors" as we described in the discussion of asynchronous control in chapter 4. The operating system, through its monitors, "owns" the resources which it loans out to the processes of the operational software systems. The operating system thus expedites the operation of "cooperating processes" but also schedules the sharing of the use of resources within the set of "parallel processes" that are currently active in the computer system: that is, those processes that are represented by programs and state variables and are currently being executed from the computer memory. In order to obtain the correct perspective, the reader should relate the operating system activities to the basic definition of processes, systems of cooperating processes and parallel processes as presented in chapter 2 as well as the control of processing presented in chapter 4.

Two basic types of operating systems are called **real time operating systems** and **time sharing operating systems.** Real time operating systems are utilized primarily in the control of physical processes as illustrated in chapter 8. In this case, the time taken to receive control signals from physical processes, to make decisions in the computer system and send out resulting control signals to the physical processes can be extremely critical. Consequently, real time operating systems are architected to adapt to the time requirements of physical processes.

In time sharing operating systems, the goal is to provide the computer system as a resource to many simultaneous users, for example, from several terminals. While it is desirable to assure them as fast access to the computer system resource as possible, the timing here is not as critical as in the control of real physical processes. The time sharing operating system permits users to operate independent of each other, that is, in parallel and without interference. Individual users can view the computer system as their own and do not have to be concerned with the fact that the operating system is **scheduling** the use of the resources for several users. However, when users do wish to cooperate in some way, the operating system serves as an intermediary for their cooperating processes.

Both types of operating systems are equipped to recognize "interrupts" which can result in the temporarily reassignment of all or parts of the computer system resources to this "higher priority process." Remember our analogy of the baby crying in chapter 2. Further, active processes in the computer system must compete for the available resources, and the operating system builds **queues** for the resources requested via its monitors. Queue building in this environment can be related to the analogy of queuing for a bus at a bus stop. The bus is a resource which has a number of places for sitting and standing and the queues assure an orderly use of the resource.

The implementation of the operating and file systems results in a number of processes which contain procedures (subroutines) that can be "called" upon by the use of a call instruction as described earlier in this chapter. Thus, these **procedures provide a "service" to higher level processes** in similar fashion to the target system providing a service to the operating and file systems, namely, the execution of their instructions. The basic notion of the hierarchy of processor-memory pairs is the **provision of services** by lower level processes to the higher level processes.

The services provided by the operating and file system when requested by "users" in a human/machine communication are requested through the use of a **control language.** These are languages in which the users tell the system what activities they want to do and when they want to do the activities. Further, the computer's operating system, as a part of a dialogue with the user, returns messages related to its own activities which are of importance to the user. Through the control language and dialogue, the user can gain access to the operating system, file system, language translators and, in fact, all available services provided by software systems.

There are many strategies which can be followed in architecting and constructing operating and file systems. Their effectivness, to a large extent, can determine the overall performance of the computer system. Many modern day single user computer systems based upon inexpensive microprocessors do not require sophisticated operating systems since competition for resources between several users does not exist. Consequently, only basic services are provided; however a good file system is important, even in this environment. The operating system for large general purpose systems that provide a wide variety of user services can be an extremely large and complicated suite of programmed processes.

Language Translator and Utility Systems

We continue the hierarchy of software processes by considering the placement of "language translator" and **utility systems** in relationship to operating and file systems and the target system as indicated in the following picture.

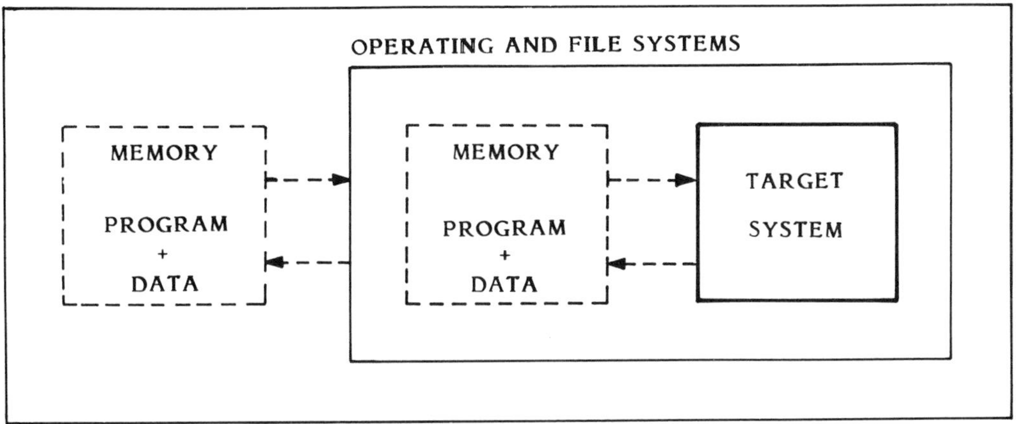

LANGUAGE TRANSLATOR AND UTILITY SYSTEMS

Again, note that the dotted line indicates that the memory utilized for containing language translators and utility systems is, in fact, the same physical memory provided by the target system. These systems simply share the memory along with all of the other software systems, including the operating and file systems.

We considered the general properties of language translation systems in chapter 6 where the translation consisted of taking a "source language program" as a sequence of symbols (perhaps ASCII symbols) and translating this program into the internal machine language (target system) representation. Various types of translators are provided for various types of languages in the computer system environment. We can categorize these into the following:

Microcode assemblers: The source program, in this case, represents a microprogram that when translated and loaded into the control memory, as indicated in the earlier picture of the target system architecture, is the program that controls the register transfer manipulation, input/output operations and memory reading and writing for the target system processor.

Assemblers: Assemblers are the language translators which were described in chapter 7 where we considered the basic structure of the cooperating processes of a computer system. The source program is a representation of instructions from the target system instruction repertoire which when translated and loaded into the target system memory become programs used to realize the higher level processes of software systems, for example, operating and file systems or even language translators themselves.

Compilers: In this case, the source program is written in an even "higher level language" than assembly language which permits us to create programs that are not related to the details of the target system. Higher level language programs are more understandable to a wider class of "users." These programs are also translated by their respective translation systems (compilers) into the machine language (target language) level for execution (interpretation) by the target system. In addition to the **general purpose programming languages** that were enumerated in chapter 6, there may exist **special purpose programming languages** for constructing the software systems programs of the computer system. Thus, a **systems programming language** is a special purpose language that contains features which are useful in creating programs for operating systems, file systems, language translators and, as will be discussed in the next section, data base systems.

All of the languages used in the computer system environment are constructed to conform to basic grammatical rules of **syntax** and **semantics.** These are counterparts of the syntax and semantics of natural languages. The syntax defines the construction rules for words from the basic alphabet of the language and the ordering of words within larger units, for example, **statements.** The semantics is the interpretation (meaning) assigned to syntactical structures.

In order to verify the difference between syntax and semantics and to demonstrate the principles of higher level languages, let us consider a source program for performing the same function as the machine language program presented in chapter 7. That is, the program reads values from the terminal until it encounters a value equal to 99, at which point it calculates and outputs the average value. We do not use any particular available higher level language but use a language notation representative of a wide variety of higher level languages.

```
PROCEDURE AVERAGE;

  DECLARE FILE (OBSERVATIONS, DISPLAY);
  DECLARE INTEGER (INVALUE, SUM, COUNT);

/*INITIALIZATION*/
  SUM, COUNT = 0;

/*PROCESSING*/
  REPEAT:   READ FROM OBSERVATIONS INTO INVALUE;
            IF INVALUE = 99 THEN GO TO FINAL;
            SUM = SUM + INVALUE;
            COUNT = COUNT + 1;
            GO TO REPEAT;
  FINAL:    WRITE SUM/COUNT TO DISPLAY;

/*TERMINATE PROCEDURE BY RETURNING TO THE CALLING PROCEDURE*/
            RETURN;

END AVERAGE;
```

The program is composed of **statements** where each statement is terminated by a semi-colon (;) and "comments" which are enclosed between the symbols /* and */. These are part of the "syntactical rules" for the language. Further syntactical elements are summarized as follows:

keywords:	PROCEDURE, DECLARE, FILE, INTEGER, READ, FROM, INTO, IF, THEN, GO TO, WRITE, TO, RETURN, END
identifiers:	AVERAGE, OBSERVATIONS, DISPLAY INVALUE, SUM, COUNT
label identifiers:	REPEAT, FINAL
constants:	99, 1
operators:	=, +, /

The reader should compare this program with the assembly language version in chapter 7. As with the lower level programs, we divide the source program into declarations and procedure processing components.

In the declarations, we do not have to concern ourselves with the details of which input/output devices, registers or memory variables shall be used for our program. The "compiler" will take care of assigning appropriate resources. In our declaration, we name higher level objects, in this case, files and integer variables.

In the procedural part, we observe the basic process logic; however, we do not have to concern ourselves with the details of data conversions from external to internal form. The compiler will "**generate**" the correct instructions when required. In fact, we can view the assembly language program of chapter 7 as a "translated" version of this higher level language program.

Notice that the program terminates with a RETURN statement which is syntactically composed solely of the keyword RETURN followed by a semicolon. The semantical meaning of this statement is to perform a procedure (subroutine) return corresponding to the use of the return instruction described earlier in this chapter. This AVERAGE procedure is available as a service to other procedures that wish to utilize it. A procedure may "invoke" this procedure with the following statement:

```
CALL AVERAGE;
```

This call statement is translated into the machine language call instruction. When executed in the calling procedure, it couples in AVERAGE as a dynamic refinement. When AVERAGE executes its return instruction, the dynamic refinement terminates and the calling procedure is resumed at the instruction ("statement") following the call instruction ("statement").

This program hopefully has given the reader a feel for the general properties of a higher level language and should have convinced the reader that it frees the programmer from being concerned with the details of machine language (target system) level programming.

Another important type of software system is the so-called **utility system.** This category includes a wide variety of programmed systems which provide important "services" to computer system users (for example, standard programs (for "sorting" of records stored on storage peripheral media based upon record keys). Such systems are normally referred to as **sort and merge systems.** Another very important utility is a **text editing system** which is one of the cornerstones of the word processing systems described in chapter 6. Editing systems in cooperation with the file system are designed to assist users in entering, editing and cataloging files of text composed of symbols (as, ASCII symbols). Consequently, the same text editor can be utilized for natural language texts and source program texts of higher level language programs.

Data Base Systems

The **data base system** is based upon the availability of the language translator and utility systems and the operating and file systems of the computer system. As with all software systems, data base systems utilize a portion of the target system memory as illustrated in the following picture.

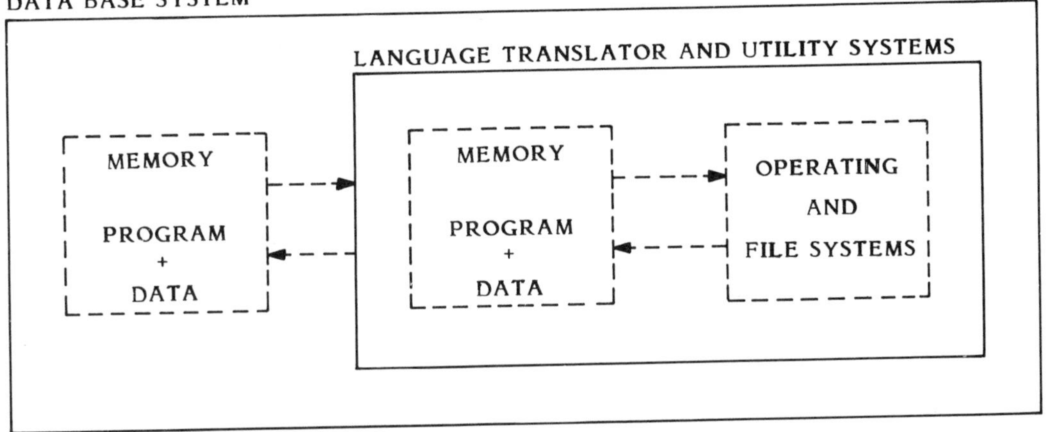

DATA BASE SYSTEM

In discussing files in chapter 8, we made an analogy to a folder and then further extended the analogy to include records as papers within the folder. We continue this analogy by thinking of a data base as one or more "file cabinets" in which the files are contained. The purpose of the data base system is to "manage" very large quantities of data. The data base system must also be organized to allow the users to make "inquiries" related to data that exists in the data base system. In this respect, the data base system normally provides for so-called **query languages** which permit the user to state the terms to be utilized in searching for the existence of data stored within the data base. The data may be the composite of data items taken from several files in the data base. Cataloging of the contents of data bases involves keeping track of the contents of all of the files in the data base. Note the similarities to manual filing and cataloging procedures used in business and governmental organizations.

Application systems

Application systems contain processes that build upon lower level system software processes and provide an interface to the **end-users,** thus providing them with access to the computer system for the type of applications they wish to utilize. Again these programs occupy a portion of the memory as indicated in the following picture.

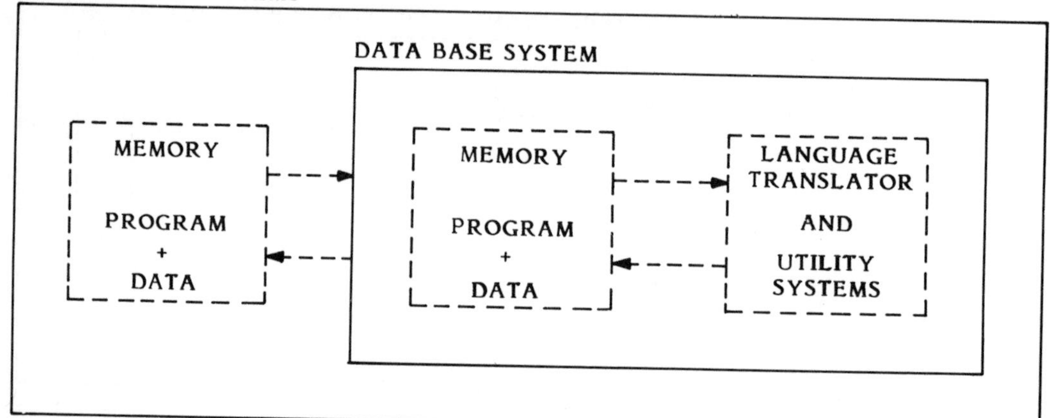

APPLICATION SYSTEMS ARCHITECTURE

In some applications of computer systems, a data base system may not be required and, in this case, the availability of language translators and utility systems plus the operating and file systems provide all of the required "services." As indicated in our earlier picture of the people involved in computer system work, it is the systems analysts and programmers that design and create these application systems.

We shall not attempt to go through every conceivable type of application of computer systems in this introductory book. The number of application categories is growing rapidly and we individuals are becoming more and more affected by the use of computer systems due to the availability of advanced application systems. However, let us consider a categorization of four major utilizations of computer systems.

Administrative Data Processing: In the business world, computer systems have made their presence known as well as in the governmental use of computer systems for processing information. It is estimated that over 80% of all utilization of computer systems is for administrative data processing. One good example of how this application area can affect us in the future is in the banking business. Perhaps someday in the future we will reside in a "moneyless society," where all transactions are recorded by computerized bank accounting systems.

Scientific and Engineering Computations: The use of computer systems for advanced scientific and engineering computations has made possible the design and development of numerical computer algorithms that would have not been conceived of in pre-computer days. The possibilities in this area can very easily be appreciated when we think about the accuracy attained in landing a man on the moon.

Real Time Control: This area was mentioned in chapter 8 and, certainly, the use of real time control and the creation of industrial robots is one of the important applications of computer systems of the future. However, we should not forget the real time control of various important resources, for example, in regulating and providing for the economic distribution of electric power. In Sweden, for example, it is estimated that the economic management of the power network by real time computer control saves the equivalent of at least one entire atomic energy plant. The use of real time control in medical electronics is, of course, of vital importance, for example, in pacemakers for the heart and in X-ray technology such as computer tomography.

Telecommunications: The advent of the computer systems was of utmost importance to the telephone and telegraph industry. Much of their electro-mechanical switching equipment could be updated to the use of "programmed processes" to provide telephone and telegraph network switching functions. This trend has resulted in the availability of high reliability telephone and telegraph systems. Further, the telecommunication companies of the world have introduced the utilization of the telephone network as a medium for transmitting data between remotely located computer systems and users of computer systems. Consequently a new industry has evolved for the telephone and telegraph companies of the world, namely, the provision of services in the form of "computer networks." The structure and applications of networks of computers will be described later in this chapter.

Architecture Alternatives

One of the important jobs of the computer architect is to assure the provision of an appropriate target system which provides a good basis for building the software architecture upon. In making the decisions, amongst many alternatives, there are several aspects that must be considered which we can summarize in the following:

performance	reliability
accessibility	complexity
flexibility	economy

The commercial sale/purchase of computer systems is frequently guided by an important purchasing criterion called the **price/performance ratio.** That is, how much performance one can receive from the computer system compared to the price that is paid for the computer system. This factor influences the architectures that are selected for utilization in constructing commercially available computer systems. The capacities of computer systems vary quite widely and computer system manufacturers provide a wide variety of systems beginning with single user systems and special purpose systems up to extremely large general purpose systems which provide service for a large number of users simultaneously. There has arisen a categorization of computer systems which is largely based upon the price and capabilities of the computer system as follows.

Micro computer systems
Mini computer systems
Medium-scale computer systems
Large-scale computer systems

Due to the major advances in Large Scale Integration (LSI) technology that were described in chapter 9, all of these computer system levels have been able to offer a continuing improvement in their price/performance ratio.

In this section, we shall consider a few of the many different ways to organize a computer system architecture. In the architecture of the model of the cooperating processes of a computer system presented in chapter 7, all input and output transfers were directed through the CPU. The CPU was "interrupted" from its ongoing processing in order to service the initiation of input/output operations as well as the individual transfers of data and/or program instructions to/from the memory. If a goal of the architecture is to increase the transmission speed from storage peripherals, particularly discs, to and from the memory process, then one may select to architect the computer system to utilize a **multi-port memory** and include a separate channel to couple the high speed storage peripheral devices directly into the memory. This architecture can be viewed in the following picture.

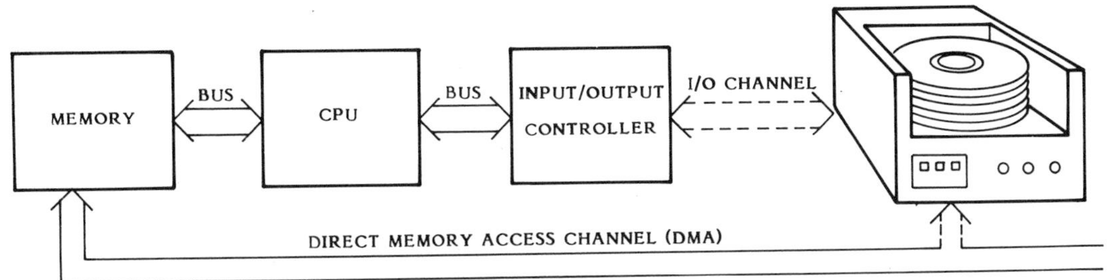

ARCHITECTURE WITH A MULTI-PORT MEMORY

Here we see that the memory process has two ports, one from the CPU which, in addition to its primary target instruction interpretation role, acts as an intermediary for the Input/Output controller. The storage peripherals (disc drives in this example) receive their commands from the Input/Output controller as to when they are to perform searching, reading and writing operations. The actual transfer of data and/or program instructions to and from the memory process takes place over a **direct memory access channel** (DMA). By incorporating this second channel which has a higher transmission speed than the basic input/output channel, one is able to improve the performance since the memory and Central Processing Unit (CPU) can continue with target instruction interpretation while the direct memory access transfer is ongoing. However, in this architecture, we should observe that there are two demands for the use of the memory process, namely, from the CPU and from the DMA. In this case, a "higher priority" is given to the DMA for utilization of the memory. We can relate this back to our earlier discussion of "higher priority processes" in chapter 2 where the baby, by crying due to wet diapers, received higher priority than the WASH and DRY processes.

If our desire is to provide flexibility in the connection of many memories, processors and Input/Output controller components into a single computer system in order to improve reliability and/or performance, then one can consider utilizing a so-called **common bus architecture** which is illustrated in the following picture.

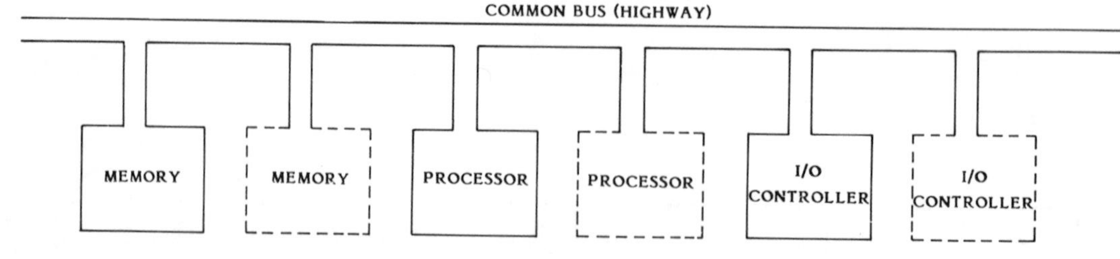

COMMON BUS ARCHITECTURE

Each process connected to the bus in this case has an address which is used to identify it to other members of the bus family. When "messages" are sent as binary signals across the bus, the messages include the destination address of the units that are to receive the messages. Each process "listens" to messages on the bus but only takes those that are addressed to itself. Individual processes can send messages to other units when they "know" their bus addresses. Thus, memory reading and writing as well as input/output transfers take place over the same common "shared" duplex transmission channel.

There are a large number of other alternatives to the architecture of computer systems. However, we should realize that as new features are added such as DMA's or a common bus, the complexity of the access to available resources and services increases. Thus, the software architecture, particularly the operating system in its role as the monitor of computer system resources, becomes more complicated. A good computer architect will try to find a proper balance between hardware and software complexity. This leads to the following definition.

ROLE AND RESPONSIBILITY OF A COMPUTER ARCHITECT

"TO PROVIDE MAPPINGS BETWEEN THE VARIOUS ARCHITECTURAL LEVELS OF THE SYSTEM THAT ASSURE CONVENIENT REALIZATIONS OF ALL LEVELS AND TO DISTRIBUTE FUNCTIONS ACCORDING TO WELL DEFINED HUMAN, ECONOMIC AND TECHNICAL GOALS AMONGST THE VARIOUS LEVELS. FURTHERMORE, TO SEEK TO MINIMIZE BOTH INTRA AND INTER LEVEL COMPLEXITIES IN ALL PARTS OF THE SYSTEM."

The Author

By mappings we mean the nature of the "objects" at one level and how they are "interpreted" by the lower levels. For large scale general purpose computer systems, the job of the computer architect is quite involved. The field of computer architecture has received additional responsibilities which are described in the final section of the chapter.

Network Architectures

In the late 1960's and during the 1970's, the pioneering efforts in the development of **computer networks** occurred. By computer networks, we mean the connection of two or more (normally remotely located) computer systems. Via the connection, the computers can exchange messages thus providing the possibility to obtain remote access to distant computer systems. Most of the early remote connections to computer systems used the world's installed telephone network as the "carrier" for the transmission of messages. There was, of course, a problem. Computer systems deal with binary signals as we learned in chapter 6; whereas, the telephone network is designed to transmit voice via the use of **"analogue signal"** representations of voice. While not the most optimal method for digital transmission, the telephone network was utilized since it was already installed. The conversion of binary signals to analogue signals and vice versa for adaptation to the telephone network is accomplished by a "black box" called the **MODEM (Modulator-Demodulator).** The limited service available via the telephone network restricted the transmission of messages to rather low speeds, for example, 110, 300, 600, 1200, 2400, 4800 or at best 9600 bits per second. This rate of speed of transmission is called the **BAUD rate.** The connections of computers as well as remote terminals via the telephone network is illustrated in the following picture.

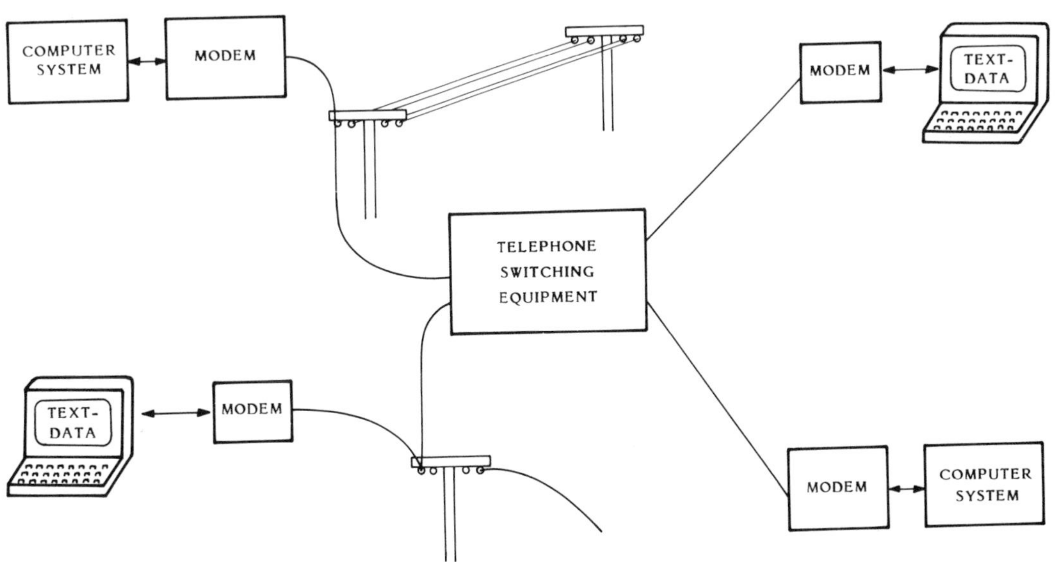

DATA TRANSMISSION OVER THE TELEPHONE NETWORK

Each computer system receives a telephone subscriber number precisely the same as individual customers. The "dialing-up" of a computer uses exactly the same method as for normal telephone calls via a conventional handset coupled to the MODEM. However, it is also possible to arrange automatic dialing procedures. That is, the computer sends the desired number to another "black box" which is in turn connected to the MODEM. While the use of the telephone network for **data transmission** is by no means optimal, it has provided a starting point for communication between remotely located computer systems. During the 1970's many computer manufacturers delivered computer network systems which provide for the connection of equipment of their own product assortment. The world's telecommunication companies, also during the 1970's, started to develop standards and recommendations for the computer networks of the future. This includes the utilization of binary signal (that is, digital) data transmission over networks that are specially designed and constructed for computer communication. These new networks will not require the use of MODEMS for digital-analogue-digital conversion.

A new industry is evolving around the merger of telecommunication and computer system technologies. The architects of the future computer networks must possess skills in computer system technologies introduced in the first picture of this chapter, as well as in telecommunication technology. In chapter 7, we considered the interfacing of processes and the utilization of protocols (i.e. formal rules or procedures) used in communication between cooperating processes within a computer system. These interfacing and protocol problems lie at the heart of computer network design. Protocols must be available to establish orderly communication between computer systems and network users.

There are two basic strategies being used in modern computer networks, namely, **circuit switching networks** and **packet switching networks.** In a circuit switched network, data is transmitted in the network at a fixed rate of speed. That is, "synchronous" control, which involves the use of a central timing mechanism as presented in chapter 4, is used to indicate the start and end points of the transmission of small data units, normally bytes.

Packet switched networks operate more "asynchronously" and include the use of buffering of larger data units (messages) when messages are produced at a faster rate than the transmission channels or the receivers of the messages can consume them. In both of these network types, we are concerned with the use of interfaces and protocols. However, only very simple low level protocols affecting the hardware transmission of data are provided in circuit switched networks. In packet switched networks both hardware and software level protocols are utilized.

The telephone and telegraph companies of the world have the authority and responsibility of providing the computer networks in the future. Consequently major standardization efforts are ongoing in this area. Unfortunately, due to marketing demands, computer manufacturers were required to provide computer networks for interconnecting their computers before standardization efforts got under way. Consequently, possibilities for communicating between various computer manufacturer supplied networks have been minimized. Further, many of the world's telecommunication companies have started to build their own so-called **"public data networks"** which provide carrier services between computer systems produced by different manufacturers. Some of these public data networks are circuit switched and some packet switched. Unfortunately, in spite of standardization efforts, incompatibilities between various operational networks remain. To solve communication problems between networks a new field of **internetworking** is evolving. Its purpose is to develop solutions to physical connection and protocol problems across networks so that a user of one network can gain access to computer resources, services and users in other networks.

As a consequence of the availability of computer networks, computer architects have started considering the possibilities of distributing the work to be performed for the users of computer systems across several different physical computers. Consequently, the notion of **distributed processing** sometimes referred to as **distributed computing** has become important. With distributed processing, for example, it is possible to retain portions of an entire data base on different physical computer systems. When a user makes a query using the query language, the distributed processing system couples in all cooperating processes, local and remote (via the network), required to satisfy the user's request.

The application of computer networks in the future will undoubtedly have profound effects upon our daily life. One can envision the possibilities of performing many aspects of white collar work from the home via a terminal. What the long range psychological effects of this change will be is yet to be discovered. As an indication of the beginning of this trend, "remote typing services" where typists work at home are developing. Another important potential information providing source is the use of the telephone network to provide information from data bases (possibly distributed) to the public. In this case, the home TV is part of a home computer system which is connected via a MODEM to the telephone network. The subscriber can make inquiries via a keyboard and, for example, select information about the news, weather, sports, securities, public events, advertisements, etc. How will these developments affect our life in the future?

Summary

There are many decisions to be made in the design and implementation of computer systems. The computer architect takes responsibility for supplying "users" with the appropriate computer system structure. In many cases **special purpose systems** and/or components may be the best choice while, in other cases, **general purpose systems** and/or components may be advantageous. In any event, there are a large number of "people" skills required in producing computer systems as illustrated in this chapter and on the cover of the book.

The majority of processes required for computer system construction are "programmed processes." At lower levels of the computer system, these processes are designed and constructed once and not altered and therefore are referred to as **static programmed processes.** Programs placed in a memory and interpreted by a processor are called **dynamic programmed processes.** Procedures of dynamic processes may be initiated by the occurrance of some event or they may be called upon by other processes as a **procedure invocation.** In the world of programming, procedures are often referred to as **subroutines.** The machine language level contains instructions for assisting in calling upon and returning from procedures, namely **procedure control instructions.**

There exist many levels of programmed processes in a computer system and the notion of nested **processor-memory pairs** is useful in helping to clarify this structure. The real physical memory of the computer system is divided amongst programmed processes, that is **memory sharing** is used such that the many processes (even of different levels) can reside in the memory at the same time. In addition to the programs for the processes, their data areas for their state variables also share the memory.

The term **target system** is synonymous with the machine language level as presented in chapter 7. In order to simplify the structure of the Central Processing Unit, it is common to utilize another lower level called the **micro architecture.** Thus, the logic of the CPU is programmed via a **microprogram** which is placed in a **control memory.** The **microinstructions** control the combinational and sequential circuits of the hardware logic. Microprogramming languages are frequently referred to as **register transfer languages.**

An **operating system** is composed of a number of processes, including monitor processes, which own the resources of the computer system and which "loan out" the resources for use by all processes currently executing in the computer system. It provides a control function for the computer system software. A **file system** is designed to provide "services" to other processes for maintaining, accessing and deleting sequential and random access files. It catalogues all files via their **file name** in a **file directory.** **Real time operating systems** are designed for managing physical processes where the response time to control the physical processes can be critical. On the other hand, **time sharing**

operating systems are designed to give service to a diverse group of users where the time of response is important but not critical. Operating systems provide for **scheduling** of the use of resources including the building of **queues** of users waiting to be granted authority for resource utilization. Access to the services offered by operating and file systems is provided by a **control language.**

Language translator systems are provided for translating various forms of source language programs into their "executable" form. A **microcode assembler** is necessary for the translation of microprograms. An assembler as discussed in chapter 7 is used for translating machine language (target system) programs. The translators for higher level languages are called **compilers.** Most higher level languages are so-called **general purpose programming languages;** however, there exist **special purpose programming languages** such as **systems programming languages** which have special features for assisting in creating system software processes. The construction of source programs follow **syntax** and **semantic** rules in a similar fashion to our natural languages. Higher level language programs are composed of **statements** and statements can include **keywords, identifiers, label identifiers, constants** and **operators.**

Computer system software normally includes **utility systems** for providing standard services to "users." **Sort and merge systems** provide for ordering the records of files according to their keys. The editing of natural language text and program source language files is provided by a **text editor system.**

The management of large quantities of data is provided by the **data base system** which uses the services of the language translator utility, operating and file systems. The data base system provides a **query language** which can be used by the "users" to search through the data base to find data of interest.

The availability of **application systems** is, of course, the main purpose of having a computer system resource. The application system provides services to the **end users.** The major application system categories of administrative data processing, scientific and engineering computations, real time control and telecommunications were described in this chapter.

There are many factors which must be taken into account in the "architecting" of a computer system. One important factor is the so-called **price/performance ratio** which is how much computing power one can buy compared to the price. There are many alternatives in designing computer systems and two alternatives were given as examples. If we wish to improve the performance by increasing transmission speeds from storage peripherals to the memory, we can use a **multi-port memory** and a **direct memory access** (DMA) channel. Another architecture, namely, a **common bus** architecture, can be utilized to provide flexibility in coupling in memory, processor and input/output controller processes into a single duplex transmission media.

During the 1970's the age of **computer networks** was entered, providing the possibility of communicating between remotely located computer systems and users. The installed telephone network has been utilized as a transmission media; however, since it deals with analogue signals instead of digital signals a "black box" called the **MODEM (Modulator-Demodulator)** is required to provide necessary conversions. **Data transmission** is provided over the telephone network according to a certain **BAUD rate,** that is, the number of bits per second.

The telecommunication companies of the world are now working on providing modern digital data transmission services through one of two approaches. **Circuit switched** networks are synchronously controlled networks with very primitive "protocols" for connected subscribers. **Packet switched** networks utilize buffers for transmitting messages across the network and are therefore to a large extent asynchronously controlled. Packet switched networks include more sophisticated protocols for hardware and software levels. These networks provided by the telecommunication companies are called **public data networks.** Unfortunately, there exist many networks which are already in operation that do not follow any standard. As a result, the **internetworking** of individual networks has evolved as a solution to gaining access to remote computer system resources, services and users tied into other networks. The availability of computer networks has provided the possibility of distributing cooperating processes across different computer systems in the network. This has led to the introduction of so-called **distributed processing,** also called **distributed computing.**

Word List

This chapter contains the essential properties of computer systems architecture that are built above the digital processes described in the previous chapter. Readers should verify their knowledge of these important concepts by reviewing the following terminology.

special purpose systems	general purpose systems
static programmed processes	dynamic programmed processes
dynamic refinement	procedure invocation
subroutine	procedure control instructions
processor-memory pair	memory sharing
target system	micro architecture
microprogram	control memory
microinstructions	register transfer language
operating system	file system
file name	file directory
real time operating system	time sharing operating system
scheduling	queues
control language	microcode assembler
compiler	general purpose language
special purpose language	systems programming language
syntax	semantics
statements	keywords
identifiers	label identifiers
operators	utility system
sort and merge system	text editing system
data base system	query language

Word List Continuation

application systems	end users
price/performance ratio	multi-port memory
direct memory access (DMA)	common bus
computer networks	MODEM (Modulator-Demodulator)
data transmission	BAUD rate
circuit switching	packet switching
public data networks	internetworking
distributed processing	distributed computing

Problems

1. Translate the AVERAGE procedure given in this chapter from its higher level language form to its target system format as instructions by selecting the instructions of the assembly language version of this program given in chapter 7 that correspond to the logic of each of the statements. Do not include the DECLARE statements. Further, translate the RETURN statement to the return instruction given in this chapter. Notice that in your "compiling" of this program a single statement results in (generates) one or more target system instructions.

2. Modify the higher level language version of AVERAGE given in this chapter so that the sum of all of the input values is displayed prior to the writing of the average value.

3. Further, modify the program so that each input value is displayed with the exception of the terminating value, namely 99.

GLOSSARY OF TERMS

This glossary is provided to enable the reader to make rapid reference to the terminology presented in this book. Every term that is defined in this glossary is followed by an indication of the first chapter in which the term was defined. Thus, for more detailed explanations, the reader can refer back to the original descriptions within the chapter and/or to the chapter summary.

-A-

access time:7: The time required to gain access to an element from a register, memory or I/O buffer.

algorithm:5: The plan for the realization of the logic of a process.

alphabet:3: A formalization of data representations in which the types of objects (data) are enumerated.

analogue signal:8: Constituted as a voltage level that is proportional to a measured quantity, for example, temperature or pressure.

analogue to digital converter:8: A peripheral device used to convert analogue signals taken from transducers from their analogue form into binary form.

AND gate:9: A gate with two input signals and one output signal. The output is 1 only if both inputs are 1.

application systems:10: A system of processes that supplies a service to the end user. The major categories of application systems are administrative data processing, scientific and engineering computations, real time control and telecommunications.

arithmetic instructions:7: Instructions used to perform binary arithmetic on numbers contained in CPU registers.

array:6: A collection of scalar objects (data) of the same basic type.

assembler:7: The language translator system utilized to translate assembly language source programs into their internal instruction representation.

assembly language:7: A low level language which provides for the construction of source programs according to the computer's instruction repertoire.

asynchronous control:4: A control strategy which attempts to achieve a degree of speed (time) independence of the rate of individual process execution.

-B-

BAUD rate:10: The number of bits per second that can be transmitted over a communication channel. For telephone based communication with MODEMS, 110, 300, 600, 1200, 4800 and 9600 BAUD are common rates.

binary digits:6: The alphabet of digits, composed of the two members 0 and 1, that is used by the computer system in representing numerical values and in performing arithmetic operations.

binary number system:6: The system of number construction based upon the use of the alphabet of binary digits.

bit:6: A term used in the computer field as an alternative to the term binary digit. Precision, for example, is frequently expressed in numbers of bits.

black box:6: The term used to describe the functions of a system component, the internal details of which are not of primary interest.

blocks:8: Subdivisions of the contents of a file. A block consists of one or more records.

Boolean algebra:9: An algebra introduced by George Boole in 1854 which only has operations corresponding to AND, OR and NOT gates and which forms the basis for computer logic.

buffer:4: A storage placed between processes that is used to hold objects (data) that have been produced but not as yet consumed.

buses (highways):7: The transmission channels used internally in the computer system.

bytes:6: Groups of bits (normally 8 bits) used to represent symbols according to a well defined alphabet, for example, the ASCII alphabet.

bytes per inch (bpi):8: The number of bytes that are recorded in one inch of magnetic tape. For example, 800 bpi or 1600 bpi.

-C-

cables:9: Transmission media used to carry control and data signals to peripheral devices.

cassette tape:8: A normal cassette tape upon which low volume sequential files can be recorded inexpensively.

cassette tape drive:8: A conventional cassette tape recorder that is connected to the computer system.

Central Processing Unit (CPU):7: The main computational and symbol manipulating process of the computer system.

character set:6: External symbol representations as seen by the human user which are converted into binary signals according to a well defined alphabet; for example, the ASCII alphabet.

chassis (rack):9: The physical structure into which several printed circuit boards (PC-boards) are mounted.

chip:9: One of the individual integrated circuits photographed onto a wafer. The good chips are selected for incorporation into Dual In-Line Packages (DIPs).

circuit switching:10: A data network design strategy which uses synchronous control for transmitting bytes (including parity bits). Only primitive protocol functions are provided for user process to user process communication.

clock signal:4: Signals given to processes in a system which assure synchronization of the processes. The frequency of the clock signal is determined from the time required for the worst case process.

combinational circuit:9: The most basic form of a digital circuit (gating network) consisting of one or more gates.

comments:7: Used to help the human reader in understanding the structure or some other important aspects of a program.

common bus:10: An architecture which permits the flexibility of adding new memory, processor or I/O controller processes in order to improve performance and/or reliability. The processes perform all of their interprocess transfers across the common bus.

compiler:10: A translation system that translates programs written in a higher level language into target system (machine language) internal representation.

complement:8: The opposite value of the current state of a memory element, for example, a flip/flop. If the state is binary 0, then the complement is binary 1 and if the state is binary 1, the complement is binary 0.

computer hardware:7: The electronic components used as processors of the memory, Central Processing Unit (CPU), Input/Output controller and peripheral cooperating processes of a computer system.

computer networks:10: The connection of remotely located computer systems and users. Early networks used the installed telephone network for data transmission but digital data transmission links are now being installed around the world.

computer software:7: Programs contained in the computer memory and in storage peripheral devices.

concurrent processes:2: A number of processes that may or may not be interrelated but are active, that is, ongoing at the same time.

conditional instructions:7: Can cause a break in the execution sequence based upon the outcome of evaluating a relationship between certain values.

configuration:7: The collection of cooperating processes in a computer system.

constants:7: Values that are fixed and which will be assigned to memory cells where their binary bit configuration will appear.

consuming process:4: A process that consumes input objects (data) produced by another process.

control:4: The system function that "coordinates" the activities of the processors as they service (execute) the processes of a system. The coordination involves the responsibility for assuring that the process activities are in "synchronization" with respect to time.

control characters:6: Special characters used in communication between the terminal and the computer system.

control instructions:7: Used to alter the sequence of instruction execution. Includes unconditional and conditional instructions.

control language:10: A language used by users to gain access to services offered by operating and file systems.

control memory:10: A memory utilized to hold the microinstructions of a microprogram.

cooperating processes:2: Two or more interrelated processes that are dependent upon each other.

cores:8: The magnetic circular elements used in constructing magnetic core memories.

-D-

data:3: A formalized representation of facts or ideas.

data base system:10: A system of processes designed to manage, as a service, large quantities of data stored on storage peripheral devices.

data conversion instructions:7: Used to convert arithmetic data from byte form representation to internal binary format and vice versa.

data processing system:3: Synonymous with the term information processing system and arises due to the use of data contra information definitions.

data structures:6: The organization of data to be processed by a computer system.

data transmission:10: The transmission of data over the available communication "channels" according to a BAUD rate.

decimal digits:6: The alphabet of digits which we human processors are accustomed to using in arithmetic: that is, 0, 1, 2, 3, 4, 5, 6, 7, 8 and 9.

decimal number system:6: The system of number construction based upon the use of the alphabet of decimal digits.

declarations:5: An enumeration of the objects of the process environment, for example, ports and state variables.

destructive write:7: The fact that the writing of new contents into a memory cell causes the destruction of the previous contents.

digital circuits:9: Combinations of gates designed by logic designers to process signals.

digital plotter:8: Utilized to create drawings, for example, engineering drawings or even computer generated art.

digital to analogue converter:8: A peripheral device used to convert digital signals from a computer system into appropriate proportional analogue signals for controlling a physical process element, for example, a motor.

direct memory access (DMA):10: A separate I/O channel used to connect high speed high capacity storage peripheral devices directly to the memory process for the transmission of data in both directions.

disc drive:8: The storage peripheral device in which a disc pack can be placed for subsequent searching, reading or writing.

disc pack:8: A collection of disc surfaces that are mounted into a disc drive as a single unit.

distributed processing (distributed computing):10: The possibility to distribute cooperating processes between various physical computer systems and to achieve interprocess communication via a public and/or private data network. A good example is the distributed processing of data base inquiries where the data bases are stored on different computers.

Dual In-Line Package (DIP):9: A capsule into which a "good" integrated circuit chip is mounted. The chip is connected to the pins of the dip by small wires.

duplex:3: Transmission in two directions at the same time (simultaneously).

dynamic refinement:10: The coupling of the program logic of a called procedure into the logic of a calling procedure. The refinement disappears when the called procedure returns (completes).

dynamic programmed processes:10: Processes whose program logic is loaded into a memory for interpretation by a processor.

-E-

ECL:9: Emitter Coupled Logic is an integrated circuit technology.

edge connectors:9: The input and output ports of a printed circuit board (PC-board).

electric signals:6: An electrical line capable of changing voltage levels.

end of file:8: A special mark representing the termination point of a sequential file.

end users:10: The people for whom application systems are designed.

error conditions:4: Indications that something has gone wrong during process execution.

external data representations:6: Data representations that can be interpreted by the human users of computer systems.

-F-

field:6: A component part of a structure (record).

field names:6: The names utilized to identify the component parts of a structure (record).

file directory:10: The catalogue of files maintained by the file system.

file name:10: A name utilized to catalogue a file within the file system.

file system:10: Provides services to processes for creating, maintaining, accessing and deleting sequential and random access files.

files:8: Collections of data and/or programs recorded on storage peripheral mediums.

finite state machine:5: The name given to a machine that has a limited number of unique states.

fixed head drive:8: A disc drive where an arm, containing a read/write head, is supplied for each track and each arm is capable of performing searching, writing or reading in only a single track.

flip/flop (latch):8: A memory element capable of retaining the state of binary 0 or binary 1 as long as power is supplied.

floppy disc:8: A thin flexible disc of the size of a 45 rpm record which can be used for random access files of small volume and which is placed into a floppy disc drive.

floppy disc drive:8: A storage peripheral in which floppy discs can be placed for subsequent searching, reading or writing.

flowchart (flowdiagram):5: A graphical means of representing the logic of processes.

full adder:9: A combinational circuit designed to add two binary digits with logic to accommodate the carry in from the addition of previous digits.

-G-

gates:9: The most basic form of digital processes which are the basis for logic design.

gating networks:9: Combinations of gates designed by logic designers to process signals.

general purpose language:10: A programming language designed to meet the needs of a broad group of users (programmers).

general purpose systems:10: Computer systems designed to meet the needs of a large diverse group of users.

graphic terminal:8: Permits the composition of pictures for display on the terminal screen.

-H-

half adder:9: A combinational circuit designed to add two binary digits without logic for accommodating a carry in.

half-duplex:3: Provides for transmission in two directions but not at the same time.

higher level languages:6: Programming languages designed to free the programmer from being concerned with the details of computer systems.

high order bits:6: The most significant bits in a group of bits; that is, the leftmost bits.

high speed printer:8: Produces printed output rapidly but in many cases with inferior quality in comparison to text typed on a good typewriter.

highways:7: The transmission channels used internally in the computer system.

human/machine communication:6: The two way communication between the human users of computer systems and the computer system.

-I-

I2L:9: Integrated Injection Logic is an integrated circuit technology which is pronounced I-squared-L.

identifiers:10: Names given to program objects in a source program, for example, file names, variable names and labels.

information:3: An interpretation given to data in a well defined context.

information processing system:3: Synonymous with the term data processing system and arises due to the use of information contra data definitions.

I/O buffers:7: Local storage of the Input/Output controller used for holding data and/or program instructions on their way into the computer system or way out to peripheral devices.

I/O channels:7: Used for the transmission of commands and data between the Input/Output controller and the peripheral devices.

I/O control functions:7: The commands given to peripheral devices via the CPU and Input/Output controller under the direction of the executing programs. The functions include reading and writing as well as a number of special control functions for particular peripheral device categories.

Input/Output controller:7: Maintains contact with peripheral devices, namely, the producers and consumers of data and programs.

input/output instructions:7: Instructions utilized to control peripheral devices and the transmission of data and program instructions to/from the peripheral devices.

input port:3: A place where objects (data) enter a process.

instruction repertoire:7: The collection of instruction types recognized by the Central Processing Unit.

instructions:7: The basic units of programs that are interpreted by the Central Processing Unit.

integrated circuits:9: The packaging of the transistors used for realizing gates.

inter-block gap:8: A separation point between blocks on a magnetic tape where no recording appears.

interface:7: The connections between two processes in a computer system.

internal data representations:6: The representation of data used by the computer system in storing and processing.

internetworking:10: The development of interfaces between two or more existing circuit and/or packet switched networks where the standards of operation in the respective networks are not compatible.

interrupt:2: The notification to a processor that a high priority process requires servicing. The processor is to temporarily suspend its ongoing activities, service the interrupt and then return to the activities ongoing prior to the interrupt.

-K-

keywords:10: Special reserved words used in a higher level language to identify important semantical aspects, for example, statement types.

-L-

labels:7: Symbolic names given to important points in an assembly language program which may be used as addresses for control instructions.

label identifiers:10: Symbolic names given to important points in a higher level language program which may be used for transfer of control from statements that cause transfers.

latch:8: A memory element capable of retaining the state of binary 0 or binary 1 as long as power is supplied.

leading edge:9: The point at which the clock signal voltage is raised.

local storage:5: Storage owned by a process and used solely for its internal operation.

logic design:9: The design of digital circuits (gating networks).

low level languages:6: Programming languages that are closely related to the details of the computer system's structure and operation.

low order bits:6: The least significant bits in a group of bits, that is, the rightmost bits.

LSI:9: Large Scale Integration with thousands of gates in the integrated circuit.

-M-

machine language programming:7: The programming of the computer system in terms of the instructions of its instruction repertoire.

magnetic core memories:8: Arrays of small circular magnets called cores which can be magnetized and are capable of representing the two binary states 0 and 1. Magnetic core memories retain their state even when power is removed.

magnetic discs:8: A storage peripheral medium used to store random access files. The binary data is recorded onto the disc surfaces.

magnetic drums:8: Storage peripherals containing a non-removable circulating cylinder (the drum) upon which random access files can be stored.

magnetic tapes:8: A storage peripheral medium used to store sequential files. The tape contains spots which can be magnetized to represent binary 0 or binary 1.

mask:9: The picture of an integrated circuit that is photographed onto the surface of a wafer.

memory (store):6: The place used to hold programs of processes to be interpreted by the CPU as well as the data of the processes.

memory address:7: A name utilized to uniquely identify a particular memory cell (word) in the memory array.

memory cell (word):7: An individual element of a memory which can contain data or program instructions.

memory cell contents:7: The contents of a memory cell; namely, the data or instruction representation stored in the cell.

memory sharing:10: The division of the real physical memory of the computer system amongst the active set of programmed processes.

messages:6: Collections of symbols entered at the terminal and sent to the computer system and vice versa.

micro architecture:10: A lower level processor-memory pair used to program the interpretation process of the target system architecture.

microcode assembler:10: A translation system that translates microprograms from their source language format into their internal representation.

microinstructions:10: The individual instructions of a microprogram.

microprocessor:9: A LSI component that contains the logic of a complete Central Processing Unit.

microprogram:10: The program that interprets the target system instruction repertoire. It is contained in a control memory.

MODEM (Modulator-Demodulator):10: A black box used to convert digital signals to the analogue signals used in the telephone network as well as analogue signal conversion to digital signals.

monitor process:4: A process that controls process access to a resource.

MOS:9: Metallic Oxide Semiconductor is an integrated circuit technology.

moving head drive:8: A disc drive where a single disc arm must be moved from track to track in performing searching, writing or reading.

MSI:9: Medium Scale Integration with hundreds of gates in the integrated circuit.

multi-port memory:10: A memory process which has more than one port. A priority for use of the memory must be assigned to the ports.

multi-processors:2: Two or more processors that are available for utilization in the simultaneous execution of concurrent processes.

-N-

NAND gate:9: A gate with two input signals and one output signal which gives the equivalent result of an AND gate followed by a NOT gate.

non-destructive read:7: The fact that the reading of the contents of a memory cell does not alter the cell contents. That is, the cell remains unchanged as a result of reading.

NOR gate:9: A gate with two input signals and one output signal which gives the equivalent result of an OR gate followed by a NOT gate.

NOT gate:9: A gate with one input signal and one output signal. The output signal is the complement of the input signal. That is, the output is 1 if the input is 0 and the output is 0 if the input is 1.

number base:6: The base used to represent numerical values; for example the decimal number base is 10 and the binary number base is 2.

numbers:6: Numerical values which can be represented in the computer system and upon which arithmetic operations may be performed.

-O-

object program:6: The internal representation of a translated source program which is in the format to be interpreted by a processor.

operand fields:7: Fields of an instruction used to name the objects that are to participate in instruction execution.

operating system:10: The "owner" of the resources of the computer system which "loans out" the resources to the concurrent processes executing in the computer system.

operation code field:7: The bit encoding used to identify the type of instruction.

operators:10: Symbols appearing in a higher level language program which specify that an operation is to be performed; for example, (=) assignment, (+) addition and (/) division.

OR gate:9: A gate with two input signals and one output signal. The output is 1 if at least one of the input signals is 1.

output port:3: A place where objects (data) leave a process.

-P-

packet switching:10: A data network design strategy which involves largely asynchronous control and where larger units (packets) are transmitted over the communication channels. Buffers are used where required. A number of protocol services are available to assist in user process to user process communication.

parallel adder:9: An adder which adds all of the binary digits of two operands during the same time period, that is, simultaneously with all required logic for accommodating carries from one position to the next.

parallel processes:2: Processes that are active at the same point in time.

parallel sequences:8: Sequences of logic that are executed simultaneously, that is, at the same time.

parallel transmission:6: The transmission of binary encodings by utilizing several signals over a single time frame.

parity bit:8: An extra bit added to a byte for the purpose of error control.

peripheral devices:7: Includes, amongst many types of devices, devices for storing large quantities of data and programs, for connection to real physical processes and to terminals and printing devices.

pins:9: The input and output ports of a Dual In-Line Package (DIP) which are connected by small wires to the integrated circuit chip.

port:3: A temporary holding place for objects (data) as they enter or leave a process.

power supply:9: A unit which supplies constant power to the computer system.

precision:6: The maximum number of binary digits permitted in processing operations of the computer system.

price/performance ratio:10: An index (measure) of how much computer performance can be purchased in relationship to the price paid for the computer system.

printed circuit board:9: A board upon which several cooperating Dual In-Line Packages (DIPs) are mounted and which has edge connectors for its input and output ports. Normally referred to as a PC-board.

printer:8: A peripheral device used to obtain printed copy of computer system outputs.

printing terminal:8: Produces printed output of a quality equal to to a typewriter but is slower than a high speed printer.

procedure control instructions:10: Instructions used to call (invoke) a procedure and to return from the called procedure.

procedure invocation:10: The calling of a procedure to be dynamically connected as a refinement to a calling procedure.

procedures:5: Units of process logic designed to perform a well defined sequence of actions.

process (task):2: A process or task is some unit of work that is performed (executed) when a processor is applied.

process control:8: The application of a computer system to the control of physical processes. In its advanced form it involves industrial robots.

process creation:2: The birth of a new process.

process execution:2: The carrying out of the step by step activities of a process.

process initialization:4: A control function that is utilized to prepare a process for execution.

process initiation:2: The starting of execution of an already created process.

process inputs:2: Objects (data) that are to be consumed and processed by a process.

process outputs:2: Objects (data) that are produced as a result of processing by a process.

process priority:2: The importance assigned to a process in relationship to all other processes. Normally determines the order of process execution.

process resumption:2: The return to execution of a temporarily suspended process.

process (machine) state:4: An indication of the current activities of a process (equivalently, a machine).

process suspension:2: The temporary stopping of the execution of a process.

process termination:2: The ending of the execution of an existing process.

processor:2: The interpreter of the step by step activities of processes.

processor assignment:2: The coupling of the available processors to the active processes.

processor-memory pair:10: The processor-memory pair provide the basis for the realization of programmed processes. Further, the nesting of processor-memory pairs is useful in clarifying the architecture of levels of programmed processes.

producing process:4: A process that produces output objects (data) for the eventual consumption by another process.

program (algorithm):5: The plan for the realization of the logic of a process.

programming languages:6: The languages used to program the various processors of the computer system.

propagation time:9: The time taken for a digital circuit (gating network) to produce its output signals.

protocol:7: The procedures (rules) to be followed in sending and receiving control signals and data across an interface.

public data networks:10: Data networks open for subscription to public subscribers in the same fashion as the telephone network. The telecommunication companies of the world are installing and operating public data networks. Some of them are circuit switched but the majority are packet switched networks.

-Q-

query language:10: A language used in conjunction with the data base system for searching in the data base to find data of interest.

queues:10: Orderly waiting lines for the utilization of resources that are currently occupied.

-R-

rack:10: The physical structure into which several printed circuit boards (PC-boards) are mounted.

random access files:8: Permits the use of record keys to identify (i.e. address) individual records and therefore permits random access to individual records within files.

Random Access Memories (RAM):7: The name given to memories where memory cells (words) can be addressed via the corresponding memory address (name) in a random manner.

read/write head:8: The mechanism of the tape drive that performs the recording (writing) or reading of the bytes from the magnetic tape. Read/write heads are also utilized in the arms of disc drives.

real time operating system:10: Operating systems that are used for managing physical processes where the response time to control the physical process can be critical.

record keys:8: Data belonging to a record which serves as a key (name) for identification of the entire record.

recording density:8: The density of byte recording on a magnetic tape as measured in bits per inch.

records:8: Subdivisions of the contents of a file. One or more records are contained in a block.

refinement:5: The breakdown of larger composite actions into smaller components.

register address:7: A name utilized to uniquely identify a particular register in an array of registers.

register loading instructions:7: Instructions used to read the contents of an addressed memory cell and transmit this value to an addressed register in the CPU. (See non-destructive read).

registers:7: Local storage of the Central Processing Unit used as temporary holding places for data being processed by the CPU.

register storing instructions:7: Instructions used to write the content of an addressed register in the CPU to an addressed memory cell. (See destructive write).

register transfer language:10: A name frequently given to microprogramming languages.

repetitive sequence:5: A sequence of actions that are repeated as long as a predicate is true; that is, while predicate; do this sequence.

resource:4: A facility that is available for usage by more than one process, for example, a buffer.

resource ownership:4: The location of a resource within a process which gives the process control over the resource.

-S-

scalar:6: An individual data item such as a number or a collection of related symbols.

scheduling:10: The operating system planning for the utilization of computer system resources that have been requested by processes.

selection:5: The selection of alternative paths of action based upon the evaluation of a question (predicate); that is, in case of predicate, do this action.

semantics:10: The meaning assigned to various syntactical constructs with respect to the context of their appearance.

semiconductor memories:8: Memories built from transistors that are used to realize flip/flops (latches) which can retain the two states binary 0 or 1 as long as power is supplied.

sequence:5: The order of performing process actions; that is, do this action, then that action, then that action, etc.

sequential circuit:9: A circuit which includes a memory element as well as a combinational circuit and which during a clock pulse, processes all or part of the memory contents and input signals to produce output signals and new total or partial memory contents. It is a finite state machine.

sequential files:8: Files retained on magnetic tapes where records are recorded one after another and are normally processed in the order in which they appear in the file.

serial adder:9: An adder which adds one binary digit from each operand during a single time frame and thus takes multiple time frames to produce a result for operands of greater than one binary digit.

serial transmission:6: The transmission of binary encodings over several frames of time using a single signal.

signal names:7: The names given to the signals used for the interface between two processes and used in the interprocess protocol.

signal propagation:9: The movement of signals through a digital circuit (gating network).

signal pulse:9: The name given to each oscillation of the clock signal.

signals:4: Used by the control function to indicate "when" something is to happen or "when" something has gone wrong.

simplex:3: A transmission in a single direction.

single board computers:9: Computers based upon the use of LSI components that contain all essential elements (memory, Central Processing Unit and Input/Output controller processes) on a single printed circuit board.

sort and merge system:10: A system of processes designed to sort the records of files based upon their record key into sequential order.

SOS:9: Silicon on Sapphire is an integrated circuit technology.

source program:6: The representation of a program in its external representation using symbols of an alphabet; for example, the ASCII alphabet.

special purpose language:10: A programming language designed to meet the needs of a small group of users.

special purpose systems:10: Computer systems that are designed to meet the needs of a small group of users.

speed (time) dependent:4: The property of process execution achieved as a result of the use of synchronous control.

speed (time) independent:4: The property of process execution achieved as a result of the use of asynchronous control.

square edge pulse:9: The oscillating voltages of the clock signal result in a so-called square edge pulse.

SSI:9: Small Scale Integration with 1 to 10 gates in the integrated circuit.

state indicators:5: Variables contained in the local storage of a process which are used to indicate the current state of the process.

statements:10: A common syntactical unit for higher level languages which corresponds to sentences in a natural language.

state transition diagram:5: A graphical means of illustrating all of the possible states of a process (machine), the possible transitions between states and the reason(s) for each transition.

state transitions:5: The movement from one state of a process (machine) to another state as the result of something happening.

state variables:5: Places in the local storage of a process which can hold objects (data). They are variables because at various points in time, the variable can have different values.

static programmed process:10: A process, the logic of which is designed and constructed and then not altered. Digital processes fall into this category.

storage:3: A place for holding objects (data) that are not currently being processed by a process.

storage process:3: A special type of process that contains a storage but in which no processing is performed.

store:6: The place used to hold programs of processes to be interpreted by the CPU as well as the data of the processes.

structure (record):6: A collection (set) of related but different types of objects (data).

subroutine:10: Units of process logic designed to perform a well defined sequence of actions.

symbol instructions:7: Instructions that are used for the manipulation of bytes (ex. in ASCII format) in order to form "strings" of meaningful symbols.

symbolic names:7: The programmer assigned names given to resources used by the program.

symbols:6: Non-numeric data that can be typed in at the terminal keyboard and displayed upon the terminal screen.

synchronous control:4: A control strategy that requires that the rate of individual process execution is completely speed (time) dependent in respect to the synchronization of all activities in the system.

syntax:10: The rules for the construction of legitimate sequences of symbols for a language.

system:2: A collection of two or more interrelated processes.

system constraints:4: Limitations placed upon a system, for example, the capacity of a buffer storage.

systems programming language:10: A special purpose programming language designed to meet the needs of constructing systems software; that is, operating systems, file systems, language translator systems, utility systems and data base systems.

-T-

tape drive:8: The storage peripheral device upon which a tape reel can be mounted for subsequent reading or writing.

tape reel:8: The reel used for containing a magnetic tape.

target system:10: The machine language level of a computer system which provides an interpreter of an instruction repertoire.

task:2: A task or process is some unit of work that is performed (executed) when a processor is applied.

terminal:6: The device through which the majority of computer system users have the human/machine communication. It is normally composed of a terminal keyboard and a terminal screen.

terminal keyboard:6: The means by which the human user communicates with the computer system. The keyboard, in addition to conventional typewriter keys, contains a number of special keys used for controlling communications.

terminal screen:6: The means by which the computer system communicates with the human user. The screen appears much like a conventional TV screen; however, it can only display symbols.

text editing system:10: A system of processes designed for the entry and editing of natural language and source program text files.

time sharing operating systems:10: Operating systems designed to give service to a diverse group of users where the time of response is important but not critical.

timing sequence:9: The driving force that controls the activities of digital circuits as provided by a clock signal.

tolerances:6: Ranges of voltage levels that are acceptable for uniquely recognizing a 0 or 1 voltage level of a binary signal.

tracks:8: The subdivisions of a disc surface where recording (writing) takes place.

trailing edge:9: The point at which the clock signal voltage is dropped.

transducers (sensors):8: Measuring instruments which measure process related features, for example, temperature, pressure, etc.

translation system:6: A collection of processes used in translating source programs into object programs.

transmission:3: The movement of objects (data) between processes in a system.

TTL:9: Transistor-Transistor Logic is an integrated circuit technology.

-U-

unconditional instructions:7: Causes a break in the execution sequence and program execution is resumed at the addressed memory location.

uni-processor:2: A single processor to be applied to the execution of one or more processes.

utility system:10: Systems that provide standard services to other processes, for example, sort and merge systems or text editing systems.

-V-

VLSI:9: Very Large Scale Integration with over 100,000 gates in the integrated circuit.

voltage level:6: Magnitude of voltage. Only two unique voltage levels are required to represent the binary digit values 0 and 1.

-W-

wafer:9: A substance onto which the logic of an integrated circuit is photographed. Several copies of the circuit are copied onto a single round wafer.

word:7: An individual element of memory which can contain data or program instructions.

word processing system:6: A collection of processes used in providing for the entry of documents, letters, books, etc. in unformatted form and which subsequently formats the text according to users' document specifications.